WHY CHANGE?

WHY CHANGE?

An Engineer's Mindset to Repair
Your LCD Display Supply Chain

KEITH MITNIK

Phoenix Press

WHY CHANGE?
An Engineer's Mindset to Repair Your LCD Display Supply Chain

FIRST EDITION

ISBN   978-1-5445-3009-3 *Hardcover*
        978-1-5445-3010-9 *Paperback*
        978-1-5445-3011-6 *Ebook*

CONTENTS

ACKNOWLEDGMENTS

Writing a book is harder than I thought and more rewarding than I could have ever imagined. None of this would have been possible without my business partner, Joe Sidoryk, who for the last seventeen years has challenged me, created a very successful business with me, and has helped develop all the philosophies that eventually became solidified in this book.

I'm also grateful to my better half and best friend, Janet Bean, who gave me such confidence and support that stepping this far out of my comfort zone wasn't as uncomfortable. Your admiration of my work alone made it worth doing.

I want to thank my boys, Sam and Ben. You put up with my work schedule when things were crazy at the beginning, but more importantly, you never appeared bored when I talked endlessly about my business. Sometimes you even thought that it was cool to write a book. Now I just hope you read it!

And finally, I want to thank all of my past and current clients that enable me to do what I love for a living.

INTRODUCTION

How's your relationship going?

In a lot of ways, your relationship with a component supplier is like a marriage. It's a long-term commitment with high stakes. You're invested in them. Their decisions, successes, and failures affect you every day.

The important aspects of a good relationship are universal: good communication, clear expectations, reliability, and cooperation. They all add up to trust and value. If the relationship is going well, you can trust your partner and you don't have to worry about it. Everything just works.

If it's not going well, you worry all the time. There are broken promises, stress, and resentment. There are unmet needs and escalating conflict. There's fallout that impacts other important relationships, too. When your partnership goes off the rails, everything comes to a screeching halt. Sometimes you can work things out. Sometimes you can't. But how do you know when it's really time to pull the plug?

Breaking up is hard to do, as they say. Everybody understands that a divorce is painful. It's messy and complicated. What most people don't understand unless they've been through it is that it's not really the divorce that hurts. The truly painful part of the process is living inside a relationship that's disintegrating. The situation just gets worse and worse until there's no way to move forward together anymore. Only when the split is finalized can you start over and create a new life. There's hope.

Right now, you might be in a supplier relationship that's disintegrating. The symptoms are very similar to the demise of a marriage: broken promises, unmet needs, stress and conflicts that are getting worse all the time. Perhaps the quality isn't up to par, the parts come in late, or you're paying too much. The components don't perform at a level that keeps your product competitive. Worst of all, the problems in that partnership aren't just affecting you—they're starting to affect your customers, too. And there's the constant looming threat that those parts might not show up at all. Your production line will go down, you won't be able to fulfill your orders, and you'll lose business.

Nobody in manufacturing changes their supply chain for fun. Sourcing components is a complicated process. With a product development cycle of eighteen months or more and millions of dollars of sales at risk, your top priorities are stability and reliability from your suppliers. You change because you have a problem and you need to solve it.

THE ENGINEER'S MINDSET

The engineer's mindset is all about solving problems in the most efficient and effective way. How do you do that? It starts with analyzing the root of the problem to find the exact point of failure. You break down complex issues to the simplest possible variables and then create solutions that can prevent the problem from happening again.

In the sixteen years I've been in the LCD display business, I've learned that there are five problems that can show up in your supply chain and only five: obsolescence, delivery, quality, performance, and cost. And these hold true not just for displays but any type of commodity. So if you're thinking of switching vendors, it means that one (or more) of these five things is going wrong for you. The key is to correct the issue or make the switch before they go *catastrophically* wrong. (There's also one thing that can go right: a new design that requires a completely new part. We'll cover that one, too.)

You may not be sure whether your current situation is salvageable, and the thought of breaking up with your current supplier and looking for a new one just seems too time consuming, expensive, and risky. You may be right! It's possible that your most efficient solution is to work with your existing vendor to address your problem. (Taking your relationship into couples counseling, if you will.) On the other hand, you might have reached the point where you just can't move forward with this partner anymore. You may feel that staying with your current vendor may be riskier and more expensive than making a change.

The decision of whether—and when and how—to end a relationship isn't easy to navigate. The process is so painful that nobody likes to talk about it. People just don't know how to decouple, and they don't know how to form new relationships well.

Precisely because it's so painful and so much work, it's worth doing right. You need a roadmap to help you make constructive decisions. When you have a systematic approach, you have a much better chance at a successful outcome. The purpose of this book is to give you a clear process you can follow to make the right call and find the right solutions. And if changing to a new supplier is the right solution, this book will help you vet and select one who can add value to your business instead of dragging you down.

In the following chapters, you'll learn how to think about your risks and needs in each of the five problem areas like an engineer and assess your opportunities in new product design. You'll discover a variety of options to address challenges with your existing vendor so you can maintain stability in your supply chain if possible. You'll get guidance to help decide when it's really time to switch. You'll learn the right questions to ask when vetting a new supplier and how to get the most out of a long-term relationship once you find the right vendor.

You'll save time problem solving and searching for solutions so your organization can get back to focusing on generating revenue instead. You can simplify your processes and reduce your risk of future problems. And you'll be able to move forward with confidence and trust in your supplier partnerships.

FINDING THE RIGHT FIT

I started out in the LCD display industry twenty-one years ago as a newly minted mechanical engineer. I worked in business development for Three-Five Systems, Inc., the largest LCD manufacturer in North America at the time. In my standard products display business unit, we served more than 400 customers, all small to mid-volume businesses. I learned a lot about the products, and I also learned all the frustrations that smaller manufacturers face when they're dealing with buying displays from a larger supplier. When you're one of 400, you get what you get, and that's about it. There may be some customization of the product itself but very little customization to the quality processes, logistics, and delivery. That kind of imbalance doesn't lead to healthy relationships between vendors and customers.

At Three-Five Systems, I met my current business partner, Joe Sidoryk. He was the director of worldwide sales, responsible for displays for Motorola cell phones. Motorola displays made up about 85 percent of our entire revenue at Three-Five, and whatever Motorola wanted, they got. As the supplier, we went out of our way not just to solve problems for our best customers but to proactively solve them in advance. It was an enormous amount of pressure because that one customer could make or break the whole company. That didn't lead to a healthy relationship either.

By 2005, the cell phone market had shifted from monochrome displays to color, and our biggest customer shifted with it. Even though the business unit I was responsible for was still profitable, it wasn't enough. Three-Five had to file bankruptcy.

I looked for a new job for about two weeks before I realized my heart wasn't in it anymore. It was so painful to pour my heart and soul into my work and have it ripped out from under me, even though my business unit was succeeding. I didn't want to experience that again. I joined forces with Joe, and we mapped out a brand-new vision for a new company.

We compared our two totally different business experiences and decided that we really wanted to offer the top-tier service that went into supporting Motorola to a broader and more diverse customer base. We defined that base as mid-volume industrial customers. We then realized that the key to stable long-term relationships is the same in business as it is in our personal life: finding the right fit. And in order to bring top-tier service to this mid-volume customer group, we could only work with the right customers while simultaneously only working with manufacturers who were the right fit for us as well. We learned to focus our business so precisely that today, we actually refer out about 90 percent of potential customers who call us. That's how important a good fit is to us, and it's the insight I want to share with you.

Beyond understanding the importance of fit, we had to understand our customers' problems. By trade, I consider myself an engineer—an engineer that is now in a sales role. Full disclosure: I would argue I never learned how to "sell." Instead, I stuck with engineering, and all we did was solve problems. I got in the habit over the course of sixteen years of asking every customer, "Why are you calling me?" We came to realize that those customer problems all fell into one of the six discrete categories. We gained experience in many different ways to solve those five problems and maximize the opportunities of new product design. These problems and solutions don't just apply to LCD displays. The process I'll walk you through can apply to any type of component in your supply chain.

That process starts with thoroughly understanding your own situation and needs. Then you can look around and see what options exist. Your best option may be to fix your relationship with your current supplier. If not, you may look elsewhere. When you have clarity about exactly what you're looking for, you won't have to speed date a hundred different suppliers to find the right one or cross your fingers and hope for the best. You can make an informed choice and move on to other things.

A PROCESS, NOT A PRESCRIPTION

Both your situation and your business are unique. I can't tell you whether you're paying too much or whether you have too many quality failures, because those are business decisions you need to make. At the same time, your supply chain problems follow a common pattern. I don't need to know the technical ins and outs of your business, because any business can follow the same process to correct those problems. I can lead you through the steps of that process, and your end result will be just as unique as your business.

As we discuss each problem in detail, you'll find that there's a certain amount of iteration built into the process. Some of the questions you need to ask or solutions you can try will be similar across different problems. That's intentional, because you'll encounter different problems at different times, and I want you to be able to use this book without memorizing it. A process isn't very useful if you start skipping steps!

Fixing problems in your supply chain is a lot of work, and there's no magic bullet that can change that. This book will guide you to the right approach so you end up in a better relationship and avoid making the same mistakes in the future. The process will make sure your hard work ends in results—because that's the goal of the engineering mindset.

The first step of the process is to diagnose your issues correctly. So let's get started by understanding the five problems (and one opportunity) so you can accurately assess your risks and needs.

CHAPTER 1

====

ASSESS YOUR RISKS AND NEEDS

Let me tell you about one of my first client experiences. When Joe and I started Phoenix Display, we had zero customers. We decided up front that we'd like more than zero. So as we started marketing our company, I approached Mary, a manufacturing buyer I already knew. I happened to already be familiar with everything about her needs: what part she was buying, her volumes, even down to how much she was paying per unit. In my head, I knew this conversation would be easy.

I targeted costs as the strongest deciding factor. I ran the math in my head and figured saving 10 percent would make Mary a hero to her company. So I called Mary and said, "Hey, I'm familiar with your company and your product. I can definitely help you out." I then offered to save her 10 percent on her displays.

"Thanks," she said. "I'll think about it."

Crickets.

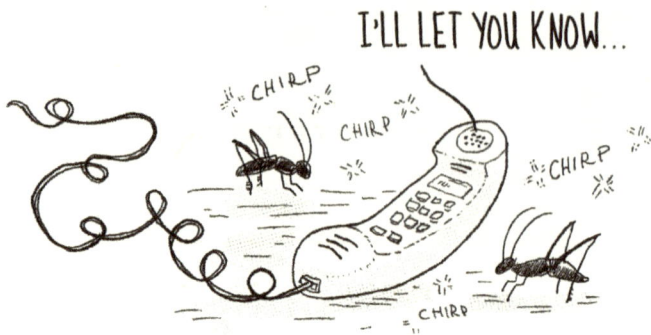

I'LL LET YOU KNOW...

Two weeks later, I called to check in with her. She said, "Yeah, we really just don't have time to work on this."

Okay. I thought maybe I should sweeten the deal. So I came back with 15 percent savings.

She said, "Thanks. I'll let you know."

Again, nothing.

I kept repeating this process until we got to 30 percent. Instead of saying yes, Mary replied, "Engineering is really busy. We don't have time to design-in your part."

"You don't have to!" I assured her. "We're going to do the design work for you. All you have to do is test it."

"Well," she said, "I'll get back to you."

Of course, nothing ever came of it. I couldn't help but think that Mary wasn't very smart. Not only that, but she wasn't working in the best interest of her company. After all, we could offer her company massive savings.

Years later, after I fully understood the impact of the five supply chain problems, I finally realized I was the one who wasn't very smart. Mary didn't actually have a problem with the price she was paying for displays. Sure, it was higher than what I was offering, but it wasn't a problem.

Sure, maybe I could have made her a hero by saving her 30 percent on those components. But what if she paid me 30 percent less and I didn't deliver? What if that 30 percent cost savings also meant 30 percent lower quality? What if switching suppliers lowered the capabilities of her product, or God forbid, they wound up going line-down because the displays didn't arrive on time?

If a company's production line is shut down due to a lack of components, that company is no longer worried about costs. They'll happily pay double the price for a component in order to keep the manufacturing line moving and maintain their customer commitments. Sure, Mary could have saved some significant dollars, but if something were to go wrong, Mary wouldn't be a hero—she'd be updating her résumé.

I had a lot to learn before I could really help customers like Mary.

THE ULTIMATE RISK: LINE-DOWN

Whether you're looking at problems with your current vendor or vetting someone new, the worst-case scenario is for your manufacturing line to go down. When you're facing supply chain issues, you're always weighing one risk against another, and the risk of being forced to shut down your production line due to a component issue (going line-down) is one of the scariest.

Electronic products require many different components, from intricate custom elements to simple connectors. If one of those components is missing, the end product can't ship. Some of those components—like nuts and bolts or a standard AA battery—can be categorized as basic commodities. If they don't show up from your current vendor, you can easily find them somewhere else.

That's not the case for more complex and customized parts like a memory chip, a printed circuit board, custom batteries, or a display. Those components are designed specifically for your product (or if you're dealing in small volumes from a large vendor's standard products, you've designed your product around the component).

Finding and qualifying a replacement for a complex component takes somewhere between six and eighteen months. It's not a fast or easy process. And if you don't have enough inventory to cover the time that it takes to design, prototype, qualify, and mass produce a replacement in time, your assembly line will have to sit and wait for it.

This puts you in a position where you have assembly workers standing around with nothing to do. You're missing customer commitments. You're missing revenue, and you may be hurting your reputation in the industry. You're allowing your competitors a prime opportunity to court your end customers. It's very, very damaging on multiple levels.

Our specific mission statement is to never let our customers go line-down. That has implications for every one of the five problems. It means meeting deadlines for design, development, and prototypes. Then in order to fulfill that mission for all of mass production, we had to thoroughly understand the five problems and get creative with many different ways to solve each of them for each and every display project that we have.

THE FIVE SUPPLY CHAIN PROBLEMS

I don't consider it my job to sell things. My job is to solve problems. And in order to solve a problem, you have to first identify the problem and then simplify it. So over the years, we've simplified everything that could go wrong in your supply chain. Every risk or obstacle that can crop up will wind up in one of these five categories: obsolescence, delivery, quality, performance, or cost. There's also one thing that can go right—designing a new product—so we include that as a sixth category.

FIVE PROBLEMS WITH LCD DISPLAYS

OBSOLESCENCE

- Difficult to plan for
- Causes significant delays in production
- Additional costs for product redesign
- Potential to drive end product to become obsolete

DELIVERY

- Number One most costly problem
- Easily shuts down assembly lines
- Reduces operational efficiency
- Missed revenue
- Missed customer commitments

QUALITY

- Damages customer relationships
- Diminishes your reputation
- Increases product manufacturing costs
- Costly product recalls or field returns

PERFORMANCE

- What is the application of the product?
- What are the necessary functions?
- The more specific performance required, the more custom the solution is
- Common problems include sunlight readability, contrast, temperature and mechanical integration

COST

Factors in Display price:
- Including functions that are needed
- Removing Functions that are not
- Optimizing display size
- Optimized LCD display integration
- Volumes

A cheaper display does not always lead to a lower cost product

...AND ONE OPPORTUNITY

NEW PRODUCT DESIGN

Problems in these areas don't always show up as an immediate crisis. They could appear first as nagging, minor hassles that escalate over time. Just like when a personal relationship isn't in crisis yet, but there are yellow flags or warning signs that things are headed in an unhealthy direction—you're bickering more, talking less, or one of you is spending a lot of late nights at the office. There are warning signs in your supplier relationships, too. We'll take a look at those warning signs and what you can do to remedy the situation before it goes downhill.

One caveat to be aware of is that identifying a problem doesn't always mean it can be solved. For instance, a customer might have a cost problem like a budget that only allocates five dollars per display, yet they've designed in twenty dollars' worth of features and aren't willing to change the specifications. In romantic relationship terms, that's like demanding a partner who has lots of experience raising kids but does not have any kids of their own. Sometimes unrealistic expectations need to be managed. The way to sort out expectations like this is to separate out wants versus needs with your vendor.

With that in mind, let's take a high-level view of the different ways the five problems can occur, warning signs that your supplier may have issues in these areas, and how the right supplier can work with you to mitigate these risks.

OBSOLESCENCE

OBSOLESCENCE   DELIVERY   QUALITY   PERFORMANCE   COST   NEW PRODUCT DESIGN

Several different situations can render a component obsolete. Perhaps the supplier has simply decided not to make it anymore due to a drop in demand below a certain level. Or they might change the design in a way that's not compatible with your product. Maybe a subcomponent within the product becomes unavailable, making the component you regularly purchase either different or no longer available.

Manufacture any product long enough, and changes like this are inevitable. The question is whether you're getting the information and help you need to deal with it up front. If you don't find out a product is obsolete until the time of order, then you're already in scramble mode. You won't have enough time to make a change before you need that part.

The key to managing that risk is clear communication and a strong relationship with your supplier. If you were dealing with a stocking distributor, they'd just pick out a similar SKU number, hand it to you, and hope for the best. A supplier who prioritizes your needs will start solving the problem in advance—when they see a component is becoming obsolete, they can hand you a potential solution at the same time they notify you of the change. The right supplier will offer you many different options to cope with the challenges of obsolescence (we'll discuss those options in more depth in Chapter 2).

DELIVERY

One of the most obvious places you'll see problems brewing is in delivery. You may not get responses as you expect. You might not receive delivery confirmations. There could be increasing variability in delivery times or missed commitments in terms of the delivery date.

When you have a good relationship with your supplier, you can call them about your concerns with delivery, and they will know exactly who you are and what you're building. They will be responsive to your situation and work with you to head off a crisis. Suppliers who have mind share at their factory can push your order ahead and get it filled quicker if need be. They might be able to ship by air instead of by ocean. If you're in a bind because you ordered a thousand pieces but you're dying for a hundred right away, they might be able to ship a partial order and get that hundred to you right away.

They should also address any potential systemic problems to head off future issues: Do the lead times need to increase? Should they create a stocking program for an entire product or for a certain subcomponent? The right supplier should be flexible, resilient, and proactive.

QUALITY

OBSOLESCENCE DELIVERY **QUALITY** PERFORMANCE COST NEW PRODUCT DESIGN

Quality issues can start to crop up as an increase in out-of-the-box failures or field failures. Quality expectations are an important part of your alignment with the right supplier. On one end of the spectrum, consumer products have different quality standards because they need to sell for lower prices, have a shorter life span, and don't see the extreme product use conditions. On the other end, the aerospace industry requires incredibly high precision and a zero-failure rate. And at Phoenix Display, we're in the middle—we build for industrial products that need to take a beating and have a long service life, but it's not necessary to build in the costs associated with the aerospace level of certifications.

A lot of people use the terms "performance" and "quality" interchangeably, but they're different. Quality refers to how well a part conforms to its design specifications. It's intended to work within certain tolerances, under certain conditions, for a certain life span. When it fails to fulfill those expectations, you have a quality problem. A supplier needs to watch for quality problems, do failure analyses, and create plans to correct and contain future errors.

By contrast, performance refers to the initial setting of the design specification for the product. So in the case of a display, that might mean brightness. If you're using a display outside and it's not bright enough to see, you might consider that a quality issue. But if that display was actually specified to operate only indoors at a lower brightness level, then the part is meeting the specifications. The quality is not the issue, but the performance is lacking.

In this example, if the end customer wants to use the product outside, we need to change the design to optimize outdoor performance. So that's the difference—performance is how well the design reflects the customer's needs, and quality is how well the product fulfills the design specifications.

PERFORMANCE

OBSOLESCENCE   DELIVERY   QUALITY   **PERFORMANCE**   COST   NEW PRODUCT DESIGN

If your customers are complaining about your product's design or you start losing market share to competitors based on functions and features, it's a yellow flag that your performance is falling behind.

Performance has a couple of different aspects. First, you want to make sure your design contains all the functions and features your end user needs and none that they don't. The flip side is that a great supplier can make your product more competitive by improving the way it serves your end customer. Suppliers who work with you on design and performance can contribute to your competitive advantage in the market.

COST

OBSOLESCENCE DELIVERY QUALITY PERFORMANCE **COST** NEW PRODUCT DESIGN

When it comes to cost, you may not see warning flags in advance. If your supplier makes unexpected cost increases, that could become an issue, but cost is not usually the number one pain point that leads to changing suppliers.

However, you could be paying too much from the beginning and you might not know it. If you see price reductions in sub-components across the board, it could be a bad sign if your custom component isn't following suit. Ultimately, it's hard to know if your costs are right without comparing quotes from different suppliers serving your industry.

Another area you could look into is whether your component is integrated with your product as well as possible, because an overdesigned or poorly integrated product is going to increase your system-wide costs. We'll talk more about reducing system-level cost in Chapter 6.

NEW PRODUCT DESIGN

NEW PRODUCT DESIGN

When you're building an entirely new product, it can be a great opportunity to form new vendor relationships from scratch, especially if your technology needs or volumes are evolving. That starts with understanding your own vision and needs.

When you're new to the dating scene, you have a lot to learn about yourself, but you probably have a vision for what type of person you're looking for. You know what makes you happy, and that gives you an idea of what a successful relationship would look like. From there, you can draw conclusions about what type of partner might meet those needs.

In order to understand what you need from a vendor, you start by understanding the needs of your end customer. What problem are you trying to solve for them?

You'll need to look at how they will interface with the product and what environment they'll use it in. From there, we can have discussions that will draw out all the different specifications you may need.

When should you start talking to suppliers about planning a new design? There's too early and there's too late. (That's the answer for everything.) It's too early before you have a framework for what the end product might look like.

For example, let's say you're designing a new doorbell system with an LCD display. What does the display actually do? How will the customer interact with it? How is that display going to make the doorbell more appealing in your marketing? If you haven't answered these questions yet, you won't have productive conversations with suppliers.

Once you've settled on who the customer is and how they will use the product, then you can start working with potential suppliers to find out your options to make that display as useful and cost effective as possible. They can help you determine variables like whether the display should be monochrome or color, how big to make it, whether you'll display images or just numbers, what kind of images they might be, and so forth.

Contacting suppliers too late in the process will impinge on the timing of your launch. If you're buying a standard product, you might need only a couple of weeks for it to be delivered. For customized solutions, though, it's often useful to have up to five weeks for just the development time during which the design can be optimized. From there, it typically takes about five weeks to produce a prototype order. You'll want to build that into your launch timeline to make sure everything is ready when you need it.

FINDING ALIGNMENT

If you're like most manufacturers, this kind of communication and collaboration may sound unrealistic. As I mentioned in the Introduction, when you're a smaller fish in a big pond, you can't always get the kind of dedicated attention we're talking about here. That's why finding the right alignment with your supplier is so important. Good alignment opens up so many possibilities for your supplier to partner with you, improve your operations, and even improve your product.

Joe and I learned the importance of alignment—and correct vetting—firsthand. At the time Joe and I left Three-Five, Inc., I had the bright idea to start my own company. I had an eleven-month-old son and a pregnant wife, and I didn't expect to make a dime for two years. I sold that attractive offer to Joe, and he liked the idea of working for ourselves and doing things differently. However, he pointed out that he also had three children and that money was in fact really helpful when it came to feeding them.

As soon as we formed the company on paper, we planned a trip to China to interview different manufacturing partners and find the right one to work with. Joe intended to look for a "real" job, but we made a deal: if he didn't get an offer by the time we flew to China, he'd join me.

As any good story goes, he got the job offer while we were sitting on the airplane in San Francisco, waiting to push back from the gate. Perfect timing. But Joe is a man of his word, so he stuck with me on the trip.

The first factory we visited was a group we had a previous relationship with. We met the general manager and about seven other senior executives in the large main conference room and we all started off very excited to work together. We made our introductions, and Joe and I gave the standard opening presentation about Phoenix Display. They gave their presentation about their history and factory capabilities.

Then after the boring formality of the old-school presentation slide show deck, their vetting process then looked like this:

"When did you start your company?"

"Last week," we replied.

"How many people are in your company?"

"You're looking at it," we told them.

That's where the meeting stopped. They told us to go back to America and work with their existing distributors to buy from them. I felt defeated. It had taken so much work just to get to this point, and these guys were basically telling us that our business wasn't viable to them.

But Joe realized they hadn't asked the most important questions. He knew that they weren't vetting us properly as potential partners. He instinctively walked up to the whiteboard, paused for a while, and then said, "How much LCD display business do you actually have in America right now?"

"Half a million dollars," they replied.

Joe wrote it up there on the whiteboard in big bold numbers: $500,000. "Guys," he explained, "that's just one customer for us. You aren't actually doing business in America yet." He laid out all of our existing relationships, our process, and our plan to only work exclusively with the right type of clients.

This fostered so much more conversation about our history, our passion, our connections, and our business plan. The amazing part is that these same factory executives who just showed us the door made a complete turnaround. They were so convinced about the value of partnering with us that they even wanted their US distributors to buy from us instead of the other way around. Sixteen years later, we still have a great relationship with the general manager of that factory. And it all came out of asking the right questions.

We took that same lesson into every aspect of our business, and we apply it pretty much every day. Because we only pursue business relationships with customers who are the right fit, we actually solve a lot of problems for manufacturers who don't ever become clients by asking the right questions and helping them get on the right path. We learned through experience that sometimes it's much more efficient to help a contact stay with their current supplier rather than working with us, and the right questions will help identify scenarios in which that's the case.

I'll give you an example. We had a new potential client that builds a very successful piece of fitness equipment reach out to us. They wanted to reduce costs. We vetted them, they vetted us, and after that, we appeared to be the correct supply chain for them. The next phase included a lot of design work on their product. Then we moved to tooling. After a few iterations over about six months, we got our display perfect and obtained our qualification on their end product.

Now that we were in the supply chain game for this end product, their incumbent supplier felt the pressure that they might lose the business to us. To counteract that, they simply reduced their price to meet ours. In the end, since the incumbent was already fully integrated into their manufacturing operations, and without a price incentive to change suppliers, the client stayed with their incumbent supplier.

The net result was that we put in six months of work and resources with no benefit. The new potential client benefited by getting their costs reduced, but that could have been achieved painlessly by simply quoting us and then sharing their strategy with the incumbent supplier. This would have avoided all the hard tooling dollars and work of that six-month process.

Conversations are much easier than cutting steel and tooling up new products. I'd always rather get in front of the true needs! It's better for everyone to do the work up front and see if there is any way to preserve the incumbent supplier relationship. That way, we get to the same place much faster and with a lot fewer resources. And if a customer *does* move forward with us, it's on solid ground. We want to be our customers' best solution, or we shouldn't be in business with them. There's no point going through all that work only to find out later that the customer was already with the right supplier the whole time.

As a company, we have unique abilities to solve certain problems, and I want to know up front if we're a good fit or not. Otherwise, just like dating, if you start off with a false impression or a fake front, it's all going to come out later on and be that much more painful. Rejection is a favor. As Warren Buffett famously said, "The difference between successful people and really successful people is that really successful people say no to almost everything."

We learned to say no to 90 percent of potential customers so that we have time for our ideal clients. That has allowed us to bring A-level service to an underserved group of mid-volume industrial product manufacturers. We create and design parts to their standard. We modify parts for them. We build for them.

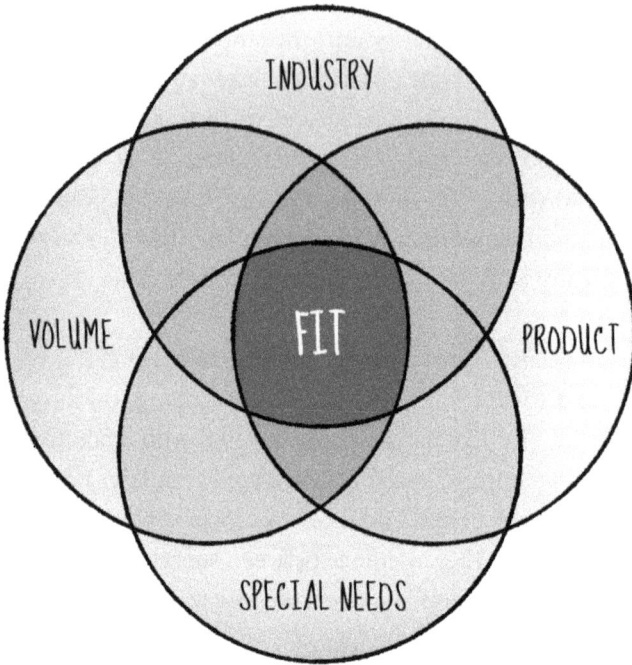

The simplest example of knowing your needs is to understand your product and whether a vendor fully supports the part you need to buy. For example, you might need to purchase high-volume computer monitors. Here at Phoenix, we specialize in small (15 inch or less) custom LCD modules, not a full 32-inch monitor. So that wouldn't be a match.

Next, you need to look for a match on volume. If you need to buy only five units, you should be working with a stocking distributor. On the other hand, if you're buying ten million units a year, you'll want to work directly with a large fabricator.

In the mid-volume range of five to ten thousand units a year, a mid-volume manufacturer like Phoenix could be the right fit.

Another aspect of fit is industry. If you're in aerospace, you'll want a supplier with experience in that industry because you'll have very specialized needs and really tight tolerances. You'll need specific quality systems and reporting in place to support you. On the other hand, if you make consumer goods, you don't want to work with an aerospace supplier because all those tight controls become far too expensive and are overkill for your needs. Consumer parts are allowed to fail sometimes. It's not a matter of life and death. And then we have industrial products somewhere in the middle—you're not paying for zero defects, but you need high-quality parts to last ten or fifteen years in the field without any problems. Wherever you fall along this spectrum, it's important that you know who you are and what you need.

It's also important to look at problems you've had to deal with in the past. For example, does your supplier need to be very responsive with lead times because your volume changes frequently? Or maybe you adjust your design every two years for business reasons, and your supplier will need to work with you to do that. These are all issues you should make a note of. Specific information like this reveals needs you might not have articulated before.

Finally, zero in on details: What is your ordering process? What unique quality constraints does your product have? What are your price targets? Where are you in your product's life cycle? Are you still in development, or do you have products in the field that might need replacement parts?

Get to know yourself and your needs so you can assess whether your current or a new supplier can meet those needs. You'll want to make sure you have this information at your fingertips when you initiate a conversation with the supplier.

ASK THE RIGHT QUESTIONS

It was only through developing the five problems framework that I realized its potential to help customers thoroughly vet a supplier. Generally, vetting a supplier is thought of as a quality audit, performed either on paper or in person. That will never determine if you have alignment with your supply chain. It will only tell you if your supplier has robust quality systems and is following those processes. That's one small part of the vetting process.

Inadequate vetting usually comes down to not understanding what to ask and not having a specific process to follow (or having a process that's not very useful). A buyer might get so focused on their current problems or the vetting process they used before that they can't see anything beyond that. Even a factory visit isn't necessarily going to tell you what you need to know unless, of course, you happen to visit on a day when there's gross negligence going on. I once visited a factory that manufactured solar panels and saw the workers washing down their clean room with a garden hose. That one was an easy pass. But the red flags aren't always waving right in your face, so it behooves you to ask the right questions.

What you really need to do is vet that supplier's ability to solve all five supply chain problems, even the ones you aren't experiencing right now, because if you decide to change, you don't want to walk into new risks and new issues.

Vetting for cost is very simple, but you can't stop there. What is delivery like? What is their obsolescence mitigation plan? What are their quality processes? Can they match or improve your product's current performance? You need to vet across all five problems every time because if you don't vet the supplier correctly, you may have just jumped from one set of pain points into a whole new set of pain points.

KNOWLEDGE IS POWER

So what's the moral of Mary's story? I didn't identify Mary's real problem. Since Mary wasn't going to change suppliers for fun, she would only change because of a pain point. Cost wasn't it. Even though there was a lower-cost option available, the cost wasn't a current issue within her product line.

I was so focused on providing a cost solution that I never even asked her about the other four potential problems, where she might have been experiencing a real pain point. For Mary, the risk of switching suppliers was much, much bigger than the benefit of saving on costs for one part. And Mary had no idea how to assess those risks.

Since then, I have learned two crucial lessons about finding the right match for a partnership between a supplier and a manufacturer. First, you have to understand the current problem (or problems) and ensure that the new or existing supplier can solve it. That problem has to have enough pain behind it that it motivates your company to take action to solve it. Second, you need a strong vetting process. That's the only way you can move forward with confidence that a change will be a change for the better.

In essence, Mary wasn't feeling a pain point that would cause her to seek out a new supplier. She didn't have a problem with her costs. The problem Mary faced was that she didn't know how to assess her risks and vet a new supplier. That uncertainty made her afraid to take a risk. She missed out on a big opportunity because of that blind spot. And we missed out on the opportunity to bring her on as a customer because we didn't yet understand how to help her.

Change will always carry some risk because it requires moving into the unknown. The process of knowing yourself and knowing your needs is how you mitigate that risk.

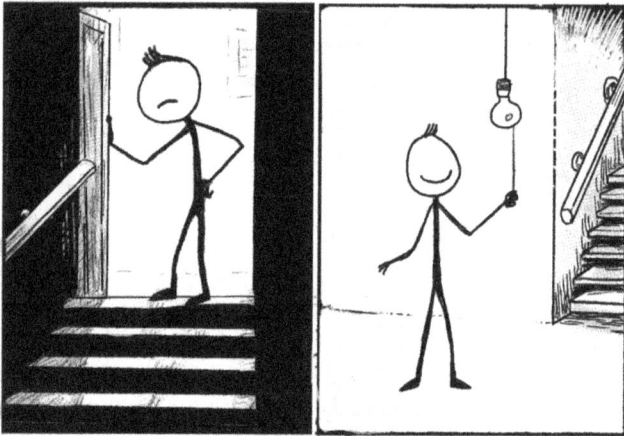

In the following chapters, we'll take an in-depth look at each of the five problems (and the one opportunity) we covered here. If you're currently facing issues with any of your suppliers in one of these areas, I encourage you to flip to that chapter and read it first so you can immediately implement some ideas that could turn the situation around.

Nevertheless, you should read the other sections as well. Thinking proactively about all your risks is the best insurance you can have against delays, crises, or encountering supply chain problems that put you line-down.

CHAPTER 2

OBSOLESCENCE

OBSOLESCENCE   DELIVERY   QUALITY   PERFORMANCE   COST   NEW PRODUCT DESIGN

One of our longtime clients is a military contractor. Their product uses a display that was designed over fifteen years ago. Now it's obsolete—it's been out of production for more than five years. They have ten thousand products in the field that are still serviceable, but as those LCD displays suffer wear and tear, hundreds were coming back. They needed replacement parts, but the parts didn't exist. These are extremely high-value items, about a $200,000 product. They were basically rotting in place for the lack of a $40 display. This client approached us to see if we could resurrect those products with a duplicate display.

Since we don't have security clearance, they couldn't share any product documentation with us. They couldn't even send us an end product to reverse engineer. To be honest, to this day, I still have no idea what the product does. I just know it's very, very useful.

DO NOT PUSH
THIS BUTTON
↓

All they could give us to go on was one working display that had been removed from a unit. From that, we were able to redesign an identical part with all-new components. It had to be 100 percent drop-in compatible because these products were already built. There was no option to alter the design or fittings on the other end.

Usually, we have specifications or other materials to help, but in this case, we had to base everything off the one working sample. We went through our Cross-Match Process (I'll talk more about that in Chapter 8), created the tooling, went through one or two iterations in prototyping, and were able to deliver them a product. These new-design replacements were able to revive all of their downed units in the field and create a lot of value for a relatively small investment.

That's not a unique story. We get these requests all the time. In the industrial market, the end product tends to outlast the technology, and redesigning an end product around a display is cost prohibitive. There are two basic stories that are typical of an obsolescence situation: availability and compatibility.

DON'T KNOW WHAT YOU'VE GOT TILL IT'S GONE

The first way manufacturers encounter obsolescence is when, in the midst of building a product, the supplier suddenly announces a part is no longer available. You're stuck. The second type of situation occurs when the part manufacturer makes a change to their product line and alters the design of your part in the process. Either way, the part you need, the way you need it, simply doesn't exist anymore.

One warning sign of impending obsolescence is an increase in lead times. When demand goes down for a component, supply will also go down; it will be harder to source and take longer to ship. As technology and industry trends shift, you may also see increases in the prices of subcomponents that get passed on as a price increase for assembled parts.

Sometimes obsolescence is based on a business decision by the vendor. Changes in the market can reduce demand for a component or a certain configuration. When sales volume for that component goes below a certain point, it's not worth it for the manufacturer to keep producing it. At that point, it becomes a specialty product that may be hard to find.

We're seeing this dynamic right now in our particular industry with the switch from resistive touch panels to capacitive touchscreens. There are fewer and fewer resistive touch panel manufacturers in the market, and that's a technology trend that's going to continue.

Another situation is when a subcomponent goes obsolete, like a particular integrated circuit, or (in our field) a particular TFT glass platform. If your supplier can find an acceptable substitute, they might make adjustments to the part to accommodate it. Ideally, the new configuration would be a drop-in replacement for the old one, without requiring any changes to your product. If that isn't possible, you're stuck again.

Often, these two scenarios create a domino effect. For example, transflective cells or certain exotic sizes of color TFT glass are very low volume. They were created for a launch customer who required enough volume to make their production worthwhile. If that original customer goes away, the market won't support continued production. The exotic item will go away, too. That market-driven obsolescence then becomes a missing subcomponent that will force your vendor to change the configuration of your part. One domino knocks down the next.

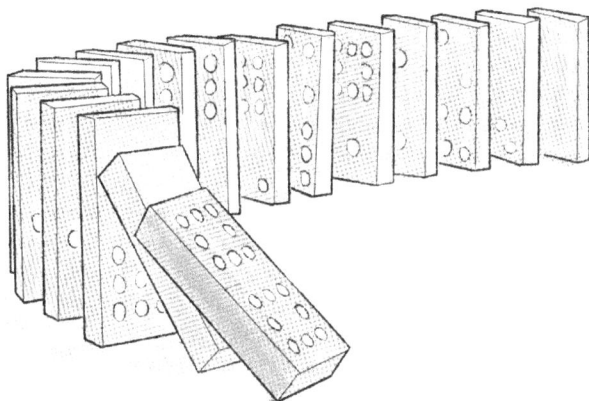

Industrial products tend to have a life span between five and fifteen years. That's a long time to be out in the field. Sooner or later, they will need parts and service. With a life cycle that long, the odds are pretty high that at least one component is going to go obsolete. That's when a robust mitigation strategy really counts.

WAYS TO COPE

As a customer, you have two basic options to cope with obsolescence. First, you could shop around and see if other suppliers are making an identical or very close replacement. If your part is very standardized, you might be able to find a drop-in replacement. That's good news! Done and done.

If you get the bad news that there isn't an exact match available, you can look for the next closest one. Then you have to compare that part against your vendor's new configuration (if there is one) to see which will integrate better with your product and what alterations you'll need to make to your product to accommodate the change.

The pain of change in this scenario is pretty high. You have to do design work to integrate that part into your product. Then you have to retool, which is even more expensive. Tooling might involve new plastics, new moldings, new metal enclosures, a new interface—you could wind up changing a lot of different components to adapt to this replacement part.

The biggest cost here is the loss of backward compatibility. You now have a new configuration for your product, and older replacement parts won't work with it. If you need to replace the obsolete component in one of your older units, you have to turn to either the spares or returns market. It's really expensive to add a new part number into your supply chain.

Of course, if your need is strictly to service existing products in the field (like our military client), you can't accommodate any alterations to the end product at all. The replacement component has to be 100 percent drop-in compatible, or it just won't work. In that case, you have to find a vendor who can create that replacement.

The first step in addressing obsolescence is having a mitigation plan in place *before* you're stuck. (I know that doesn't help much if you're stuck right now, but you can be prepared for next time.)

Your plan starts with cataloging your needs. Then you'll examine your supplier's process and see what measures they have in place to avoid problems or keep those problems from impacting you.

YOUR NEEDS

You need clarity on the expected life of your end product. Compare that to the expected life of your components. Then take a look at your complex components and investigate what circumstances or market forces might render them obsolete. If your product lifetime is long enough, every part will go obsolete sooner or later. Your aim is for the lifetime of your components to be longer than the life of your product.

If you discover that you're likely to lose a key component along the way, consider whether it makes sense to proactively change your design and incorporate a different part with better longevity. If you find that certain low-volume subcomponents are the weak link in the chain, start looking around for more commonly used options. As a general rule, I advise clients to avoid specialty subcomponents in their design wherever they can. That exotic configuration might lend itself to a better overall product design, but more often than not, the hassle of replacing the component later won't be worth it. A more readily available standard component will often give you an even bigger benefit in the long run.

Sometimes obsolescence creates an opportunity for you to redesign and relaunch your product with a new concept. If you're struggling to find 1980s replacements for a big, thick CRT monitor, it's a strong hint that you should be building something different. A sleek mounted wide-format flat-screen monitor is easier to source, and it will bring your product into the current century. That obsolescence is a signal that it's time to change your tastes to match the market.

YOUR SUPPLIER'S PROCESS

The next step to a mitigation plan is finding out the supplier's process. How much notice will they give when they stop making a part or change their configuration? Six to twelve months' advance notice is a reasonable expectation. A vendor who offers top-tier service will notify the customer of changes as soon as they find out themselves.

Find out what measures the supplier takes to avoid making their products obsolete and what measures they take to reduce the impact configuration changes will have on you. Manufacturers are component customers as well as suppliers, so they will also see their subcomponents go obsolete, and they need to be prepared for it.

A top-tier vendor will notify clients of an upcoming obsolescence and then begin an internal design process to figure out how they can solve this problem for their customers. Then they can offer a range of solutions and recommendations including the deadlines to make a final buy of the old configuration. You'll receive that formal notice at least six to twelve months prior to the last-time buy. The notice will also include the last-time order date for this soon-to-be-obsolete component and a last-time delivery date (typically two to six months after ordering).

In addition to a proper last-time buy notice, a top-tier supplier will give product replacement options. These options might include an existing identical replacement component or plans to retool and replicate a close match themselves. Adapting to a replacement part is much easier when your vendor collaborates with you and absorbs as much of the change as possible on their end.

Sometimes you may wind up with a small interface change that can be adjusted with a minor software update. Vendors who take responsibility to make those close matches and software adjustments help their customers keep consistency through their supply chain, saving a lot of effort, time, and money.

One of the key decision points here is making sure that you have enough stock of the original component while you are designing and qualifying the replacement. Any gap between running out of the obsolete component and the introduction of the new option will put your production line down—and that's the very thing we want to avoid!

If an alteration to the component is too difficult to incorporate, then your only option is to create enough margin to ride out the manufacturing lifetime of your product. The vendor might be able to simply add stock of the pre-obsolete component. This strategy works particularly well when the subcomponent cost is relatively low with respect to the overall costs. For example, you could make a risk-buy agreement with the supplier so that they purchase three years' worth of this subcomponent. That would give you three more years of uninterrupted production at a lower investment cost to transition to your next-generation product on your own timeline without any extra redesign costs.

The keys here would be accurate planning and adding safety margin to your last-time purchase quantities because if three years actually turn into four, you can't afford to run out of components. You'd need to plan for spares and repairs as well.

RELATIONSHIP ISSUES

We had one customer who came to us very unhappy with their supplier. Every six months, they'd get blindsided by another design change to their display. There was no notice, no discussion, and no planning. The product just showed up different, with a super-helpful note that read, "Here's the updated part number." Every time, this customer had to suck it up and deal with it. They wound up redesigning their product four times over the course of a few years.

HERE'S YOUR APPLE!

Ultimately, issues like this with a vendor are just like issues of trust, shared expectations, and accountability in a personal relationship. You need to rely on your partner to have your back and watch out for your interests. You need a mutual understanding of how to communicate and address problems. And you need your partner to take responsibility for helping to make the relationship work.

TRUST

I find that in general, a lack of trust will often prompt me to meddle in someone else's job. Right now, for example, I have a redesign project going on at my house. I'm getting way too involved in the details, and I know that means I lack trust in the people I hired to do it. I'm not an interior designer. I'm terrible at it, and I don't really want to jump in and pretend to be an expert somewhere I don't belong. Instead, I need to examine whether my discomfort is based on something concrete, or if it's just my own impatience and a founded or unfounded lack of trust with the process.

You should be able to rely on your supplier to be the expert in their products so you can stay in your lane and be the expert on your product. If you build medical pulse oximeters, you shouldn't have to learn all the ins and outs of building LCD displays, too. If you feel like you have to jump in and study the details of a whole separate industry, it's a big red flag that your supplier might not be doing their job to solve your problems the way they should. Your twenty years in your industry, plus one month studying LCDs, can never replace the twenty years I've spent working in my industry, and there's no reason you should try.

A strong relationship of trust with your supplier allows you to benefit from their expertise and advice. You need to be able to rely on their knowledge and skill, just as much as you need to rely on them to be consistent and follow through on their commitments.

EXPECTATIONS

Vendors of different sizes and in different industries will naturally have different approaches to how they handle obsolescence. The important thing is that you know what to expect. Your vendor should set clear expectations with you about their process and then meet those expectations consistently.

Those expectations include the timing of change notices and time frames for placing final orders. They include knowing your account rep and who else (if anyone) you should talk to about issues with configuration changes. They also include the parameters of how much problem solving, design work, and collaboration they are willing to do in the event of an obsolescence. Are they going to put in the effort to ensure that an alternate subcomponent will work seamlessly, or are they just going to drop it off and say, "Good luck"?

The worst story I hear from customers—and sadly, I've heard it multiple times—is when they've suffered from an immediate obsolescence with little to no warning. In our industry, changing suppliers can be done in as little as six months, but with all the testing and qualification, it's usually a nine- to twelve-month process. It's a serious commitment, and most product manufacturers in our mid-volume market typically manage only a single supplier for each component. So when your sole source for a part suddenly dries up, there's no backup. The damage is significant.

There are two main causes of a situation like this. Sometimes it's because the supplier just has really inadequate processes supporting obsolescence and notification. More often, it's because the customer is in the wrong level of the distribution chain.

When you buy through a stocking distributor, you don't have any configuration control and you're several layers removed from the original manufacturer of the part. So notifications may not get to you in time (if they get to you at all). When the manufacturer stops producing your part and the distributor's stock runs out, it's just gone.

I see customers who've been producing something for years frantically quoting every supplier they can. The one and only question they ask is, "When can I get this part?"

I explain my process, and often it's just too long for them to wait. They're line-down today, and even at top speed, our process takes six months to do right. I feel bad for their predicament, but I feel even worse because right now, they're not vetting for any of the other supply chain risks. They aren't looking at performance, quality, or future obsolescence. Cost is out the window because they'll pay anything at that point. It's a terrible situation, and they just don't have the luxury of time to do all those assessments.

They aren't stupid, and they didn't bring the situation upon themselves. They got let down, and now they're in a bind. And to make it even worse, those desperate decisions in a moment of crisis can set them up for even more problems down the road.

ACCOUNTABILITY

If you're already stuck with an obsolete part, you need to know specifics about how to adapt the replacement to your product. If both additional customization and tooling will be required, is the supplier willing to do the work? Who picks up the costs? A top-tier supplier will be your guide on what is best for you before, during, and after their part becomes obsolete.

Now, what does it mean to be proactive *during* an obsolescence? It's not common, but I'll give you an example. One of the contributing factors to the integrated circuit (IC) shortage in 2021 was a series of natural and man-made disasters. An IC fab burned down in Japan. Typhoons in India. Flooding in China. And most of all, work shortages due to COVID-19.

A supplier who is truly proactive will follow up with their own subcomponent vendors to see how these major events might affect their supply chain. Sometimes those fabricators rebuild and can resume operations after a pause. Sometimes they go out of business. A supplier who cultivates open communication and good relationships in their own network will have more options to keep those disruptions from affecting you.

If a supplier has a varied and agile network of vendors to acquire identical subcomponents, interruptions like this might only cause some temporary delays and lowered output. If they don't have that backup support or if the break in production is long enough, they might wind up discontinuing or reconfiguring a part altogether. The only way to know the depth of your supplier's network is to ask. Open communication with your suppliers is a strong hedge against uncertainty. The depth of these subcomponent relationships is critical as well. When these now-hard-to-come-by components go on allocation, who gets first dibs at them?

You already have a lot to do to keep up on industry trends for your own end products. It is much, much harder to keep in touch with trends for all your various components and sub-components from other industries as well. That's why you need to be able to lean on your supplier to have proactive, long-term conversations about your product's life cycle and designing for longevity. Ask these questions. They should have good answers. If not, that's a red flag that they're not in tune with their own industry and they're not prepared to fully support your needs.

THE RIGHT TIME TO CHANGE

When is it time to pull the plug and change to a new supplier? That's a business decision for you, of course. But you don't want to leave it too late. That customer who redesigned their product four times to deal with constant repetitive obsolescence could have saved themselves a lot of hassle if they started looking to replace that supplier a bit earlier.

If you've received notice of obsolescence and your supplier's not providing you with a solution, you have to make a choice about whether to invest in a last-time buy with them and how much stock to purchase. If your product life still has ten years left, you probably aren't going to buy ten years' worth of components. Whatever amount you decide to buy, with a ten-year time span, you will be in the open market looking for a new partner at some point.

You've decided that you'll continue building your product.

You've decided that a last-time buy to provide for your product's entire life cycle is too extreme. You have to come up with another solution. Regardless of whether the part is going to disappear completely or if there will be changes that will cause compatibility issues, you need parts. If you had a good experience with your current supplier on the other four problems we'll discuss in the upcoming chapters, then the path of least resistance is to revet your current supplier and see if they can be part of your new direction. Sometimes obsolescence just isn't your vendor's fault, and you can still have a successful relationship in the future.

In that scenario, if your supplier is providing you with a solution, how good is the solution? How well is it integrated with your product? How challenging are the adjustments you'll have to make on your end? To truly assess the usefulness of their proposed solution, you would need to get a second opinion. It's similar to selling a house—when you have only one offer, you have no way of knowing if it's too high or too low. You want to wait until you get a second offer so you can begin to understand what your options are.

Integrating a replacement part is going to involve a certain amount of work on your end either way, so you might as well entertain a different solution from a different supplier. Bringing in a new part is already hard, so it's not that much more effort to contact one or two other suppliers and ask what they can do. Making those inquiries is worth your time. That's when you'll see new ideas and new options. Reaching out for alternate quotes is the best time to vet new suppliers for their obsolescence risks (and the other four problems, too). Your process with a new potential supplier will encompass the same points as your mitigation plan with your current supplier.

VETTING A NEW SUPPLIER

You need a good idea of how communicative and collaborative the alternate suppliers are. Asking all these questions will show you a lot about their response times and how thorough they are in answering you.

Talk to the suppliers about longevity. Ask them about their mitigation plans, how clued in they are to industry trends, how well prepared they are to adapt to those trends, and where their parts fall in relation to the movement of the market—are they cutting edge or on the verge of being outdated? Are they designing with the most up-to-date materials to get the longest lifetime run of the part?

Discuss what changes in subcomponents, manufacturing, or the industry at large might make their parts go obsolete. What can they do about it? How much notice do they give, and how much assistance do they offer to make the changes seamless to you? Ask whether they have a stocking program to keep supplies of a particular subcomponent just for you.

Ask about the part you currently need and whether they can recommend a drop-in replacement. If not, find out as much as you can about the closest match. How much effort will it take to integrate that part, and can they help with redesign? It's crucial that you're realistic about how much change your existing system can handle—not only within the product but also in your manufacturing process.

The more out of date your obsolete part is, the harder it will be to find or build an exact match and the more subcomponents your new supplier will need to substitute and reintegrate. A supplier who is well aligned with your business can absorb much of that impact on your behalf, but they can't always eliminate it altogether. Every adaptation introduces costs into your system, and you need to know the limit of when those adaptations are worth making or not.

Find out who else this replacement part is being built for. If it's built for a lot of people, you need to know what kind of volume is supporting that production and how often they make changes. If it's built specifically for you, ask how changes are initiated and qualified. When you're getting custom items, you have the opportunity to test and qualify any changes to the part before they're put into production. That should never be a surprise.

When you decide to move to a new supplier with a completely new part, you start to circle back to some of the same questions you'll encounter with a new product design, so it will probably be helpful for you to review Chapter 7 on new product design as well. The upside of doing extensive redesign work is that you encounter all sorts of opportunities to increase efficiency and reduce waste. A well-aligned supplier will give you a realistic assessment of where your design features increase costs, so you can decide whether they're worth it to your bottom line.

NEVER SETTLE

When we served a giant customer like Motorola in their heyday, they expected (and received) white-glove treatment. That kind of individualized attention isn't always available to mid-volume manufacturers, so let me pull back the curtain a bit to show you the benefits of good alignment with your vendor.

First-class treatment from your supplier means they can react quickly and thoroughly to an obsolescence situation. When every product is aligned to the customer, your needs come first. Everything the supplier does is motivated by adding value for you. They look for ways to improve your product and its manufacturability, to increase your reliability, and decrease your system-level costs.

Here at Phoenix Display, if a subcomponent we use goes obsolete, we proactively source the closest possible match. If we need to change the configuration of our product to absorb the new subcomponent, we take responsibility for that change so our customers experience the least impact possible. We want everything to stay the same for them in terms of color, optical performance, electrical, and mechanical and anything else that is critical to their design.

In most cases, we absorb the tooling cost and supply them with a notice. Then a few weeks later, we offer them a part to test and qualify. If there's a risk of a gap in our own supply chain, we communicate that to the customer and take it upon ourselves to stock up on that component. We may ask for some liability coverage on the extra stock, but the whole purpose of these plans is to prevent an obsolete subcomponent from putting our customers line-down.

When we qualify a replacement part, we aim for "as good or better." The goal is to make a seamless match, but we always open up the conversation to ask if there are any enhancements or adjustments that would make the customer's life easier moving forward. There might be a design change that would make the end product easier to manufacture. We'll walk the customer's manufacturing floor and talk to some of their assembly people to find out any difficulties they have like "I can never connect it on the first try because this cable is too short." Since some changes are happening anyway, this is the ideal time to ask for the wish list of anything that might enhance the end product.

We plan our supply chain and manufacturing to prevent any of our products from becoming obsolete. We make long-term commitments to support our customers and their products and do the behind-the-scenes work to keep those commitments.

Once you've solved the problem of your part being available and compatible, you still have to get those parts into your facility. And they need to show up reliably, on time. So let's move on to discuss how you can address problems with delivery.

CHAPTER 3

DELIVERY

OBSOLESCENCE   DELIVERY   QUALITY   PERFORMANCE   COST   NEW PRODUCT DESIGN

One of our longtime customers is a design house for an industrial products manufacturer—let's call them IPM for short. We supply them with displays, and we've never put them line-down.

Two years ago, IPM got stuck in a supply crisis due to another vendor. One of their proprietary components went into allocation. It wasn't obsolete, but the vendor's production slowed down to the point that the highest-value orders were getting shipped first, and everyone else just had to wait. They couldn't get any deliveries; they couldn't even get an order confirmation. They're building a very high-volume, very valuable product. Their worst-case scenario happened: they went line-down.

No matter what type of product you're building, timely delivery of every component is critical.

Let's imagine you're building a point-of-sale terminal. Your manufacturing line is moving, and you have assembly workers all down that line. If you're missing a part, what happens?

Nothing.

That's the problem! The whole production comes to a grinding halt, and nothing else can get done until those parts show up.

Now you have workers sitting around with nothing to build. You're losing efficiency by the minute. Beyond that, you're missing customer commitments. When you break those commitments to your customers, it creates knock-on effects to their relationships with their own customers. Your POS terminal doesn't get to the distributor. The distributor can't deliver to a restaurant. The restaurant that was counting on those terminals has to go back to reading the servers' bad handwriting on paper tickets. Some poor guy with a shellfish allergy winds up in the hospital.

A long line of people are counting on you, so you have to count on that delivery.

Your customers don't want to get stuck any more than you do. In a case where this happens, a customer might cancel on you and move to a competitor who has the inventory on hand. Worst of all, it damages your most valuable asset: your reputation.

Once IPM got through their immediate crisis, the CEO laid down the law: "I never want to see that happen again." They began a proactive review of their entire supply chain to create disaster mitigation plans and ensure they would never go line-down again moving forward.

Even though the original problem had nothing to do with us, we were happy to work with IPM on their review. Our mission statement is to never let a customer go line-down, and this review took our contingency plans to the next level. How could we create even more product availability insurance for this customer?

We already keep safety stock for IPM. We already have the option to expedite shipping from ocean to air. On top of that, we took some critical components and second-sourced them, just in case our normal source failed us. This exercise made our own supply chain much more robust and responsive.

And it was a good thing, too! As it turned out, 2020 happened, and the global viral pandemic led to the "great chip pandemic," with a worldwide shortage of integrated circuits (ICs). At the same time, it just so happened that the COVID-19 safety precautions being put in place everywhere made IPM's product incredibly popular. In the first three months of the pandemic, their volume increased twelve times over.

A massive increase in volume can strain your supply chain even in the best of times. This was *not* the best of times. Manufacturing in China slowed to a crawl. Lead times doubled. So did shipping by ocean—vessels were parked in the Pacific trying to get in through the Port of Long Beach. Our components were still getting made, fortunately, but it cost twice as much and took twice as long to get them here.

This is exactly what a disaster mitigation plan is put in place for.

So we snapped into action. We stocked finished inventory in China. We added stock at our facility here in Phoenix as well. We improved our shipping options to minimize costs. We got in front of as many orders as we could with the safety stock in Arizona so that we could ship by ocean as much as possible without holding up a delivery.

And it worked! Our customer got the displays they needed from us, and their other vendors were able to step up, too. They filled their orders. Their products were deployed in more public spaces than ever before, and they helped the world stay a little bit safer.

I love this story because IPM took initiative to engage with their suppliers ahead of a problem. They had a scare, so they took action to make themselves stronger at every point in the chain. Then, when an even bigger crisis hit, they were prepared to cope with all the new demands of a completely unprecedented situation. The way you prepare when things are good can see you through bad times and vice versa; the way you respond when things are bad have the opportunity to make you an even better company in good times. When you win, you win; when you lose, you learn.

A MATTER OF TRUST

Delivery is a very simple problem that's easy to understand: will your order be correct, complete, and on time, or not? Late deliveries are the number one red flag that your supplier is becoming unreliable.

Problems with delivery damage your supplier relationship, just like an unreliable partner is going to tear up a relationship in your personal life. You need to be able to trust that they will show up on time, when they said they would. They also need to show up wholeheartedly, not in a half-assed way, just like your orders need to be complete, not partial. Broken promises break trust, and that always erodes a relationship over time.

Delivery isn't an issue that crops up after the product is finished and ready to ship. Organizing reliable, timely delivery starts at the beginning. When you start talking to a new vendor, building trust in their delivery process begins with the quote. What expectations do they set for both delivering the quote and for their design process overall? Is it a reasonable time frame, and does it work with your production or launch schedule? Most importantly, do they meet the target?

Delivery is not just about receiving mass production parts on time. The same standards hold true throughout the design and tooling process: is the vendor reasonable, clear, and timely in delivering designs and prototypes? All these steps demonstrate how reliable the vendor will be for delivery in production. They also allow you both to get started with mass production on schedule so you'll have your part when you need it. We use this "new product development" phase as a "getting to know you" phase. By the time we deliver the qualification samples, there would have been so many deliverables from design work, technical feedback, prototypes, qualification testing support, product design iterations, and finally qualification unit production that our customers will know exactly what type of supplier they are dealing with.

COMMUNICATION

Good communication and clear expectations help prevent trust issues. They can also show the vendor's good-faith effort when things go wrong. Your relationship with a supplier isn't a one-time deal, like buying a used car. You both need to be invested in the health and sustainability of this partnership, because unlike the one-time used car purchase, this is a multiyear mutual-dependency relationship.

Just like with a date, there's a big difference between getting a call that there's been a change of plans and being stood up. An excellent supplier who's the right fit will give ample notice of any potential delays so you can plan around them. For example, you might be able to set up your assembly line for a different product in the meantime. A partner who keeps you in the loop helps ease the burden of an unavoidable delay.

Another variable to look at is what caused the delay. Was it something within the supplier's control, or was it due to outside factors (and if outside factors were involved, how predictable or unprecedented were they)? Was it a situation that the vendor could—and, arguably, *should have*—been prepared for? You should expect your suppliers to cope with normal events without making them your problem. A global chip shortage is an extreme situation. A key person being out sick isn't.

Finally, look at how much effort your vendor puts into trying to overcome delivery issues. You need to be able to count on a partner to try everything they can to support you. That support might include brainstorming solutions for you so you don't have to scramble or absorbing the extra cost to expedite a delayed shipment. If they can't meet their commitments, how much are they willing to invest in making things right?

CAPABILITY

When you encounter difficulties in delivery, you need to look back at your needs and find out how (or whether) you can get those needs met with the current supplier. That's often a matter of the manufacturers' capacity and your actual volumes. As with the other four problems, it's always a question of finding the right fit.

If you are a supplier's largest customer, for example, five times larger than the next, then your demand can be at the high end of what they can handle; they may struggle to produce enough volume within your time frame. Maybe their factory is spread too thin with multiple small projects, each with their own setup times and support needs. It's very common for suppliers to serve more customers than they can handle. Often, they lack the discipline, the strategy, or both for choosing the right customers and planning for growth. This is typical of many companies, as they view each incremental new customer strictly according to the potential revenue they could bring, rather than addressing the longer-term high opportunity costs associated with a non-ideal customer. When you begin to exceed five times larger than the other typical customer they serve, the potential exists that their facility is just too small, and they don't have the capacity to support your volumes. The Apple iPhone and your treadmill may both have displays, but based on volumes alone, their needs—and facilities that will support them—are entirely different.

Keep in mind, your supplier's capacity could limit your own capacity for growth—if they can barely meet your needs now, how can they possibly keep up if your business were to double?

The flip side of that is a mismatch where your volume is too small to be significant to the vendor. If producing small volumes for you hurts their efficiency, or if a larger customer ups their order, your shipment is going to get bumped.

There's a sweet spot where you matter to the supplier, but you aren't the 800-pound gorilla that sucks all the air out of the room. We typically like to see factories run no greater than 85 percent capacity per year. A vendor that's running at 100 percent all the time doesn't have any flexibility or room to grow—or more importantly, have the bandwidth to actually focus on you.

That sweet spot for you, as a customer, is to be in alignment with the same volumes of their other clients. Again, you don't want to be the customer who orders a thousand units a month if the same vendor is shipping ten million a month for the iPhone. These are different business models that require different types of factories altogether. You also don't want to be with a supplier that is trying to serve both. I refer to this as you don't go to a Chinese buffet and order the pizza. Because once the gorilla's needs show up, you no longer exist. It's also hard to have the same systems and support in place for two such radically different manufacturing styles.

Sometimes delivery issues show up because things are going really well. Your volume may increase suddenly due to a big new order. You might need to double your order for one month but not permanently. Now it's not so much about the supplier's total capacity but their agility. These are good problems to have, but they still need to be solved. You need your supplier to be flexible and responsive. Perhaps they can break up your order into partial shipments to get back on schedule or meet an accelerated deadline.

If you're normally ordering 5,000 units a month, you aren't actually going to use them all on day one. Perhaps your supplier could send 250 units per day until you're caught up. There's a big difference between having your order show up short and planning for multiple smaller deliveries—which comes back to having good communication and responsiveness.

A vendor you can trust is a partner who demonstrates that they are willing and able to work with you and put in the effort to meet your delivery needs and get you the results that you are looking for. Now let's look at some of the practical changes you and your vendor can make together.

A RIVER RUNS THROUGH IT

When the water in a river is low, all the rocks are exposed and become hazards. When it rains upstream, the water level rises. Then it can flow smoothly over the rocks. A dangerous, bumpy ride on the rapids turns into stable, steady progress. In terms of delivery, the "rocks" are obstacles and gaps in your supply pipeline. Adding extra inventory and flexible shipping options raises the water level upstream from you and smooths out the flow of your supply chain. Good communication helps you steer a course around any big rocks you still see in the river.

The "water level" is the amount of inventory you have available for your assembly line. Raising the water to the right level starts with the supplier having a robust supply chain of their own. It depends on their production capacity and schedule, where you fall in their priority scale, their ability to physically get the parts to you, and their ability to hold safety stock for you. You need to take all of these factors into account when you do your resource planning.

PRODUCTION

A lot of times, production delays are caused by a subcomponent in the vendor's own supply chain. Just like you, we can't build our products without all the parts. So you want to make sure your supplier has strong relationships with their own vendors and second source key components when appropriate so that they don't go line-down either. When you and your supplier are well aligned, you can ask for this type of review, just like IPM asked us.

PRIORITY

Manufacturing priorities are another inflection point where your vendor can make it rain and compensate for potential delays before they affect you downstream. They may be able to reprioritize orders to make sure a customer who's in a bind gets their order fulfilled first. They might add shifts to the production schedule to speed up their output. That's why it's important to have mind-share with your supplier so you're not just a number and you get their attention and consideration when you need it.

SHIPPING

A delivery system has to be flexible and resilient. In our business, shipping via ocean is the default. About 80 percent of LCD displays are made in China and almost 100 percent from Asia. That percentage will vary a bit according to the component you're looking at, but the majority of electronics come from Asia. We consolidate orders into large shipments and move them to the United States in the most economical way to move products so we can increase value and pass those savings on to our clients.

Normally, shipping from Asia takes four weeks. That lead time becomes a lever because, if need be, we can cut four weeks out of our delivery schedule by shipping via air. Your vendor should keep you apprised of potential delays and offer flexible shipping to keep your line moving.

STOCK

If one subcomponent presents an ongoing problem—say the normal lead time is eight weeks, and this one particular subcomponent has been taking twelve weeks to show up—a vendor can stock up that particular component and pull from stock to get back to a normal lead time. In the same way, safety stock at many different stages of production creates extra layers of insurance. For Phoenix, we can keep buffer subcomponent stock at our China facility and keep finished goods buffer stock in both our China and our Arizona facility. Depending on the nature of your business, we recommend our clients hold safety stock as well.

A common guideline is two weeks' worth of stock at the supplier and two weeks' worth at the customer's facility. That creates enough margin to handle variations in supply and demand and smooth out some of those rocks in the rapids of your manufacturing flow. This helps clients support some unforecasted upside demand as well as protect against unforeseen manufacturing delays. We call this manufacturing insurance.

It's a careful balance. You don't want to invest too heavily in inventory because that incurs costs and comes with a risk of obsolescence. You might stop producing your product for other reasons or make a change to your configuration, which would result in a glut of useless components. You also need to consider the cost of capital. The more cash you have tied up in your parts inventory, the less you have available for other things.

PLANNING

Materials resource planning (MRP) or enterprise resource planning (ERP) means having the correct lead times in place for all the different components you need. If your suppliers' lead times are changing or if you never had the correct lead times in your system in the first place, you need to update your system to drive your orders accurately. For instance, if your vendor's lead time has increased to ten weeks on average, and your MRP system is still set to eight weeks. Your order process will only drive you to place material orders eight weeks in advance, and based on the actual component lead times of ten weeks, these components will be two weeks late each time. Additionally, remember that an average ten-week lead time means by definition that half are less and half are more than that amount of time. So depending on the manufacturing lead time variation of this supplier, you may need to add one to two weeks to the ordering process to ensure that 100 percent of the time the components meet your manufacturing schedule.

So if you frequently find yourself expediting orders, you can adjust your MRP to compensate. If you're a month off all the time, your correct margin should be one month's worth of safety stock. You're looking for ways to add more water to the river.

Maybe that's stocking full components. Maybe it's a specific subcomponent that lowers the cost of inventory. Making sure your MRP is correct in both lead time and safety stock helps you raise the water level for yourself.

Sometimes a customer has to plan for a worst-case scenario. In Chapter 2, we looked at obsolescence situations and discussed the importance of knowing whether your system can tolerate any changes in subcomponents. If your tolerance is low enough, you might choose to make a last-time buy of that particular subcomponent. Now you have a new set of risks and tasks to store and manage that inventory. Electronics are perishable.

The closer your components are to a finished state, the less protection they'll need. A finished display can be stored for about ten years before the connectors begin to oxidize, while you shouldn't store an IC for more than a year. If you're storing anything for a year or longer, you'll want to house it in an environmental chamber where the temperature and humidity can be controlled. Improper storage or just holding stock too long will result in lower manufacturing yields from your order.

Another aspect of planning for timely delivery comes into play when you work with a new component on your existing product or in a whole new product design. The process of qualifying and integrating that part takes time—sometimes up to six months. A client may not be able to wait for that process, plus a normal order and delivery time. So we look for ways to bridge the gap and make sure the subcomponents we need are on hand to start building as soon as possible.

For example, we might risk-buy subcomponents. Our custom

and semi-custom products are typically built with some standardized subcomponents, like glass and connectors (I'll discuss the reasons for that in Chapter 7). Before we have a fully qualified configuration, we'll identify which of our subcomponents have the longest lead times, and if the dollar risk is low or the part is deemed to have a low risk of changing, we may opt to go ahead and risk-buy production quantities of these long lead time subcomponents prior to qualification. After all, if we're planning an initial run of a thousand units and we need to preorder a fifty-cent connector, we're risking only $500. That's a no-brainer if we can shave three months off the project. Planning according to demand and risk-buying subcomponents are two ways to keep delivery times from putting you line-down.

A PARTNER WHO DELIVERS

Change is hard. Sometimes in the short term, it seems easier to keep your head down and take the hit from those rocks just to keep moving forward. But when you have inefficiencies in your manufacturing or you're constantly scrambling to compensate for a supplier's shortcomings, it costs real hard money. If you need to stock six months' worth of a component to make up for unreliable delivery, that's a huge cost of capital. It can sound esoteric to say that "we change when the pain of change is less than the pain of staying the same," but the calculus starts with dollars and cents.

Your own time and energy have value as well. The amount of effort you put into compensating for delivery problems steals your attention from the rest of your work. There's no reason to live with delivery problems because they can be solved in any situation. You shouldn't be in pain all the time.

You should not be living with constant expedites. They're costing you time, money, and headaches, and it's all so unnecessary. There are so many tools, from safety stock to better forecasting, that can raise the level of that river. When you are aligned with the right supplier, you can take trust, communication, and flexibility for granted.

So let's say your parts arrive on time, in the right quantities. Now it's time to open the box and see how well your vendor is meeting your quality expectations.

CHAPTER 4

QUALITY

OBSOLESCENCE   DELIVERY   QUALITY   PERFORMANCE   COST   NEW PRODUCT DESIGN

If you're reading this book, you're most likely trying to resolve a component issue by improving the performance of your supplier or finding a new supplier. And if you're involved in that process, it's more likely that you are either in Supply Chain or Engineering. Either way, supplier quality may not be your passion or expertise.

I get it; it's not mine either. We aren't recommending that you become a quality expert, nor are we recommending that you forgo the process of supplier quality audits. But you should expect ongoing quality support and performance from a supplier in order to maintain a good relationship. It is possible that a supplier can pass an audit and have all of their ISO processes in place and still not support you. In this chapter, we'll focus on that support and what it should look like to the engineer or supply chain professional.

One of our clients builds an automotive display product with a touchscreen. We'd been running one particular part for them in production for over five years. Suddenly, we started getting field returns on products after six months of service. We were not seeing these failures at our final testing, nor did our client see any of these failures in their out-of-box testing or their final product tests. Field returns are the worst and most damaging type. They are dramatically more expensive because getting the part back from the field is costly and time consuming. Even if the components are replaced at the manufacturer's cost, the effort of getting the part out of the product and replacing it requires a huge amount of time and labor. On top of that, the cost and inconvenience to the customer risks damaging the manufacturer's reputation.

At first, we thought usage conditions were the issue—the product was being used outdoors, there was humidity, maybe the end user was cleaning the display with a caustic product, something like that. But the quantity of returns started going up and up until it finally reached about a 20 percent failure rate.

Quality engineer or not, we can all determine that that's not going to be good for business!

When we analyzed the returned parts, we found the fault between the layers of the touch panel and the flexible circuit board. We'd never, in the history of our business, seen that particular fault with such a high failure rate. There could be one or two from a production lot, but never anything as high as 20 percent. And the latency of the failure made it even more challenging to define the root cause.

We started by looking for patterns of usage that could have contributed to these failures, and nothing added up. We looked at all of our process records to see whether anything in our manufacturing was out of spec. It wasn't. We asked the client if anything had changed in their configuration.

Nope.

The only clue we had was that all these returns were from the same touch panel manufacturing lot. Between time in the field until failure (six months), the client's assembly process, their logistics, our stocking the logistics, the ocean shipping, and the manufacturing lead time, those touch panels were actually manufactured over a year ago. So we had to just use data to trace back that far to see what went wrong.

Since all the units actually passed final testing, there were no clues there. So we followed our process logs on that particular manufacturing lot until we got to the bonding stage. (If this book were all about product quality, I would have a whole chapter on the importance of manufacturing lot traceability so that you can even do this sort of analysis.)

For the touch panel manufacturing process, the flexible circuit board is bonded to the glass with a conductive adhesive for a specific amount of time, pressure, and temperature. We studied the flexible circuit component, the glass, the top layer PTE touch panel substrate, and spent considerable time studying the lot of the conductive adhesive that mechanically and electrically bonds these components together. We found no issues with any of these subcomponents. We also found that with each subcomponent, there were components from the same lots that were also used in displays that did *not* experience any latent failures.

With materials removed as the source of variation, we turned back to the touch panel manufacturing process itself. All of our process parameters, assembly operators, and quality managers are documented for each lot. This allows us to go back over a year and try to unwind the story of how this happened.

Well, it turned out that the bonding time for this particular batch was on the low end of the range. It was within specifications, but that slight variation was the only common factor we could trace that affected all the failed units.

Bingo! We finally had a concrete deviation, and now all we had to do was correct it and, just as important, make sure we had containment.

To tell you the truth, I didn't like our findings. The variation in the soldering process was so small, and this process isn't usually that sensitive. It was a weak theory, but it was the only data point that made any sense. We were shipping tens of thousands of units per year to this customer, so it's not as if we were going to let this slide. Better to err on the side of caution than let our customer down. We pulled the serial numbers of that entire manufacturing lot and recalled and replaced them all before they had the chance to fail in the field and cause more damage.

We took corrective action and changed our specifications so that the bonding time remained closer to nominal. At the same time, we reviewed all other lots to ensure that they were bonded using the nominal sure times. Then we went into containment mode and monitored all of the subsequent lots going out into the field to make sure our fix actually fixed it. As the newer lots reached that six-month mark, we knew they had all been built at nominal. If the bonding time was the real problem, they should be okay.

Slowly, new failures started coming in as the next lot of displays approached the six-month in-field time frame. This shows the importance of containment—had we not been both vigilant and capable of lot traceability, we could not have been certain that these new failures were outside of our failure mode theory.

Getting more field failures was bad, but it would have been much worse if we didn't understand the true reality behind these failures. The containment data showed that the touch panel lots with the full cure time were failing in exactly the same way as the touch panels manufactured on the low end of the cure time. This means that the quality issue was not contained, and our initial cause of the failure mode was not correct. Therefore, the corrective action was not a resolution to this quality defect we were seeing in the field.

We turned the red alert back on. This investigation wasn't over; back to square one.

We went back to the beginning again, which means more conversations with the customer about their assembly process and their end product. Had anything—anything at all—changed?

Come to find out, yes. They had introduced a new configuration, but because it connected and operated with our part in the same way, they didn't think it was important. And the nail in the coffin on this one was that we had one lot of two thousand displays that straddled the two configurations evenly. With the original configuration, our part had not one single failure. And with their new configuration, we had a 20 percent failure rate.

With zero failures on the older design, and a high rate of failures on the new product, it was now abundantly clear that the customer's changes were somehow contributing to the problem.

Time to get the CSI forensic squad involved—the material scientists. We had to go over every component that they had changed, on every level. We finally discovered that the new configuration used a different material for the gaskets that held our displays in place, and the outgassing from that gasket material contaminated the flex-to-glass bonding material on our touch panels. After six months of exposure, these bonds started to fail.

Our customers are our partners. We always walk in assuming the problem is ours, until it's not. If we just threw up our hands and said, "It's not our fault; we built this correctly," what could they do to fix any problems that arose? Our client can't analyze our components or track the data on these parts the way we can. And even when, as in this case, it's not our problem, it's still our problem until it's fixed. And since it's our component that is failing, a client still needs our expertise on how their assembly would be adversely affecting our component. It's not about assigning blame—these supplier-customer partnerships only work if our customers are able to have successful products in the market, so we just want to solve the issue and get them back in business.

DEFINING QUALITY PROBLEMS

When we talk about quality issues, we're talking about two discrete types of problems: out-of-the-box failures and field failures. They can have different causes, and they impact your operation in different ways.

The first type of quality issue shows up on your assembly line. Either a part is visibly damaged, or you assemble it into your product and discover along the way that the component isn't correct. Depending on how far you've built the end product, you may have to go back and disassemble the whole thing to remove the faulty part from your line.

The part then goes to your Materials Review Board section to take it out of production and is then eventually returned to the supplier for replacement or credit. This isn't an overly complicated process. It happens with every vendor and customer to some extent.

If the number of out-of-the-box failures gets too high, it can become quite costly. You'll wind up with a lot of units being built twice. The return and replacement process takes up management time. Significant amounts of failures can affect your overall output: if you need to build 2,000 units and your order yields only 1,500 working parts, then you're short to your end customer, and with a potential eight- to twelve-week component lead times, that stock needs to be made up somewhere else if possible. This kind of quality failure is expensive and damaging. The other kind is much, much worse.

FIELD FAILURES

As with the story about our automotive client, let's say you've already shipped your product to the end user. Then, for some reason, it doesn't work or stops working long before its life cycle should be over.

The hassle and expense of getting that product returned and replaced really depend on the type of end product, of course. A cheap handheld calculator is less costly to replace compared to something more extreme like a failure in the International Space Station. That's a big deal and very difficult to correct. And because of these extremes, it is actually not possible or practical for your supplier to be responsible for the costs outside of replacing the defective product. The way your supplier will pay is long term: if these field failures continue, they will lose you as a client.

In addition to replacement costs, field failures that hit your reputation and future sales are always a big deal. If your products don't work reliably, your end customer is going to find ones that do. That loss is real, so field failures are typically the most painful for your business.

CAUSES OF QUALITY PROBLEMS

A number of factors can contribute to quality issues from your vendor. As we discussed in Chapter 2, complex components contain many different subcomponents. In the case of LCD displays, it could be up to thirty or forty. Each of those subcomponents has nominal specifications and a range of tolerances for each specification. So you wind up with tiny variations from one subcomponent to the next, commonly referred to as the tolerance stack-up.

If all the subcomponents in an individual part wind up on the far end of the tolerance range, it can cause the whole component to wind up out of spec. Or you might have one particular subcomponent that's completely out of spec, and it puts the finished part out of spec, too.

Every manufacturing process has tolerances as well. Let's say a manufacturing tool gradually gets out of spec due to usage, and it's not checked or calibrated on time as it should be. Then your component is going to wind up out of spec as well.

Improper handling can introduce quality issues to the part after it's built. As the part comes off the line and goes into its box, it needs to be protected. The clean room needs to be run correctly (you know, like *not* being washed down with a garden hose). Damage can occur in shipping, particularly if the packaging isn't robust enough for the type of treatment international shipments are subject to.

The component also needs to be handled and stored correctly. For example, a high-humidity environment can cause issues with exposed electronic traces. Even if your finished product can handle high humidity, the unassembled components probably can't. Electrostatic discharge (ESD) is another common component killer. Proper grounding can protect these components from ESD caused by simply handling the parts. There are so many opportunities for a quality failure along the way.

PROCESS VERSUS PEOPLE

My least favorite excuse for quality failures in production is "operator error." Actually, I don't believe in operator error at all. Yes, people build things and there's a natural variation from one human being to another. But I believe that errors in production come from the process, not the people. A manufacturer's process has to be strong enough to support the fact that people are individuals, not robots (even if they're building robots), and they have variation. That variation needs to be built into the process for the process to be considered robust.

My go-to example of this concept is McDonald's. Arguably, they're one of the greatest companies in the world just because they are so incredibly consistent. They open on time, every single day. Their products are identical throughout the world, across forty thousand stores. And although you may not actually like their product at all, you know exactly what the product will be because the process results in every single unit getting manufactured exactly the same way across each store. They do all this with lower-wage employees, while experiencing about 300 percent employee turnover per year.

They use some of the least experienced workers you could find, with no specialized skills. Their training is minimal compared to an industry like ours. So how do they achieve such extreme consistency? Process. They've made their process so simple that almost anyone can do it. It's documented so clearly that anyone can follow it without making mistakes. And their facilities are designed to seamlessly support the process.

As McDonald's clearly demonstrates, simplicity, excellent documentation, and support make a robust process that isn't subject to operator error. Any manufacturer whose process is so complex it requires a PhD to follow is going to get a larger amount of variation and errors in their product—even if they're hiring PhDs to execute it.

The same is true in the business side of the operation: if a purchase order wasn't transacted correctly or a report wasn't done correctly, then we need to fix the process to ensure that mistake won't happen again. Because if nothing changes other than slapping an employee on the wrist, that error will show up again and again. Most people genuinely want to do a good job, but we're all human. A vendor can't fix errors by fixing people; they have to fix their process to get results.

QUALITY VERSUS PERFORMANCE

Back in Chapter 1, I mentioned that many people confuse quality issues with performance issues, and sometimes you have to take a closer look to discover which one you're really dealing with. Every attribute of a component has specifications with their own nominal values and tolerances.

When your part doesn't perform according to its specifications, it's a quality problem. It doesn't do what it's supposed to do as well as it's supposed to do it. If the component meets its specifications, but if those specifications don't meet your needs, then that's a performance issue. If it's a performance-related issue, then the part wasn't originally designed to do what you need it to do. As long as the parts still meet the specification, the issue isn't quality related.

An everyday example would be comparing a Ferrari to a Honda on a racetrack. Is the Honda lower quality because it won't win the race, or is the Ferrari lower quality because it can't go a hundred thousand miles with minimal service? Neither! These are both examples of the product meeting the intended specification. It's a difference in performance.

A good example of this in my field is backlight brightness. The nominal value for a display's luminance might be 300 nits. A customer might be dissatisfied because it's not bright enough when used in direct sunlight. The user may infer that the display is low quality. But a 300-nit display is really designed and intended for indoor use. You'd typically need a minimum of 600 nits for outdoor viewability. So the quality is fine, but the customer has a performance issue.

On the other hand, if the display was designed for outdoor use with a 600-nit minimum and it was producing only 300 nits, then it's a quality problem. The product isn't performing within its specified limits.

Sometimes failures are actually due to the end product design and the component integration, which makes them even more difficult to diagnose. In this case, the end product itself is causing the damage to the component. That's when you wind up having to do detective work, like we did with our automotive customer.

Another example is when the end user operates the unit outside its normal environment. Extreme heat and humidity or extreme cold can go beyond the limitations of an integrated circuit or even the LCD itself and cause damage or dramatically reduce the life of that component. It's important that the environmental rating of the entire end product does not exceed that of any single component within that product.

WORKING WITH YOUR SUPPLIER

If your personal relationship isn't living up to your expectations, the first thing to do is talk to your partner about it. Perhaps you love to travel, and at the beginning of the relationship your partner always came along. You had a great time together, and they seemed really enthusiastic.

Then, as time goes on, you notice their enthusiasm for travel just isn't there anymore. Your partner still shows up and sees all the sights with you, but it feels perfunctory. You aren't enjoying your vacations anymore because you can see they aren't enjoying them either. You're not living your best life together.

The quality of your relationship has changed.

Naturally, you ask your partner what's going on. Your partner confesses that they never enjoyed traveling. They just put up with it for your sake. They're willing to continue making the best of it, but they can't fake their feelings anymore and they just aren't going to be good at that aspect of life anymore.

So what do you do? Can you accept that your travel adventures are always going to come with a side order of martyrdom from now on? Maybe you can adapt to the situation by traveling solo or with friends. Or maybe, if it's very important to you that your partner shares your interest, it might be time to split up and find a different partner. Similarly, when the quality in your vendor relationship goes off the mark, the first thing to do is have an honest conversation about it: are you still aligned, and are there ways you might adapt or work through the issues?

Nobody else can dictate your personal deal breakers in a relationship, and I can't tell you exactly what threshold of quality failures qualifies as "too many." You have to define that for yourself based on your own operations and business goals. But when you're facing too many out-of-the-box or field failures and the underlying cause has been properly identified, the next thing you need to do is find out whether your vendor is willing and able to correct it.

You need to find out what type of corrective action they can take and how they plan to contain the problem in the short term with the existing product. Can the product be reworked, or does it need to be replaced? Is there a product sort involved and where does this sorting happen? Is it on your production line, or does all of the product go back to your supplier?

Then you need to look at the long term and determine how they can work with you to mitigate future problems. After all, when the intention of this relationship is to live happily ever after, saying sorry isn't enough. It doesn't make everything better, and it doesn't ensure that whatever happened won't happen again. Sorry is just a starting point. The problem still needs to get fixed.

The proper response to a common failure is a failure analysis and subsequent corrective action. The most typical format is an 8D, or eight-disciplines, report. The purpose of the 8D (or similar report) is to create a defect resolution process, because clear processes offer a much higher probability of consistently meeting our goals.

The 8D starts with forming the team to find and correct the

problem. The team then describes the problem and defines exactly what went wrong. They implement an interim corrective action to stop the problem from proliferating. Then they investigate the root cause of the issue, develop and implement permanent solutions, and put preventative measures in place to keep the problem from recurring.

EIGHT DISCIPLINES (8D)

D1: Create the team.

D2: Define and describe the problem.

D3: Develop interim containment plan; implement and verify interim actions.

D4: Determine, identify, and verify root causes and escape points.

D5: Choose and verify permanent corrections (PCs) for problem/ nonconformity.

D6: Implement and validate corrective actions.

D7: Take preventive measures.

D8: Congratulate your team.

Looking back at the example of our automotive customer, our interim containment plan was to recall and replace the entire lot of displays. The permanent corrective action was changing the specifications for bonding the circuit board to the glass.

Then comes the containment to ensure that the entire corrective action plan was effective in eliminating this defect. The plan (which is typically the same across all failures) was to monitor the serial numbers going out post corrective action, which meant the product should be improved. Then we looked for failures and reperformed the investigation as necessary. We worked with the customer by monitoring all future field failures, and then by performing traceability analysis on each product failure, we tied it back to the specific date of manufacture of the failed touch panel. Now the guessing game is over. Once you have a failure from a component that was manufactured after the corrective action is in place, you know that the failure was not contained and the corrective action did not fix the problem.

Your dialogue with your vendor will reveal several very important clues about your relationship. First, how organized are they? Are they responsive, timely, and clear in the way they communicate with you? Are they physically organized at their factory? You may not be a quality expert or an expert in the subcomponent your vendor builds, but you're an expert at getting things done correctly. A chaotic, sloppy factory is going to perform very differently than a controlled, well-run facility. Although the organization of your supplier does not guarantee their quality will follow suit, a disorganized facility more often than not will not have the processes in place to support your needs. You may have a lower cost component coming out of a disorganized, lower-end facility, but if this comes with additional quality defects, your overall system-level cost to produce and support your product will actually be higher despite the lower component price tag on that component. (We'll go into that further when we discuss costs in Chapter 6.) Putting it bluntly, sloppy organizations build sloppy products.

Next, how much effort are they willing to put into eliminating the errors? Are they truly engaging with you in the investigation and corrective process, or are they just responding with an apology and promising that it will never happen again? Or maybe they're telling you that this error rate is acceptable to them and it will not change.

Can you live with that?

If you can't rely on help from your vendor to mitigate quality issues, you may be able to catch and contain field failures on your own by increasing the scope of your reliability testing. We test our parts to 300 percent of their specified tolerances before we ship them out, but this testing could really be done anywhere. These tests include:

- Mechanical critical dimension testing
- Electrical testing
- Optical testing
- Burn-in tests by operating the product for sixty hours
- Elevated temperature tests that put the part at 60°C for 240 hours
- Vibration testing
- Design and development product drop testing on all six sides
- Vibration and drop testing inside the product packaging to make sure the packaging does its job

If you're doing extensive testing as part of your production line, you'll want to test to a lighter specification to avoid wearing out the parts prematurely. But adding extra tests can help you avoid more expensive problems down the road. Depending on the type of tests and your requirements, many of them can be pushed upstream to your supplier to reduce the burden on your facility.

TIME TO CHANGE?

The right time to change suppliers for quality issues is essentially the same answer as for any of the five problems: when the pain of staying is greater than the pain of changing. If you can work things out with your supplier or take action yourself to get the issue under control, I'd always encourage you to try that first. After that, it's just an economics problem.

Step one of the answer to that math problem is evaluating the options you might find with other suppliers.

VETTING FOR QUALITY

Everyone needs different things from a relationship, just like every customer is different in what they need from a supplier. A process of comparison will lead you to a partnership that can meet your needs.

When you reach out to new potential suppliers, discuss your needs and the quality problems you're currently facing. Be clear about what's going wrong, your quality expectations, and acceptable defect rates. Discuss your end user and their environmental conditions, such as extreme heat, cold, humidity, or UV exposure.

Ask potential suppliers the same questions you asked your current vendor about their correction and containment processes. Let them know about any special requirements you may have for your quality standards and what your current supplier did (or didn't do) to meet them. Use this opportunity to assess their responsiveness, communication, and organization—just like you did with your current supplier. How would this new supplier address the same scenario that is happening with your current vendor?

Then you'll move into an audit process. If you didn't thoroughly audit your current supplier or if those audits are out of date, you might want to revisit these items with them for comparison.

Start with the QA audit. If it's done virtually, we'll call it a paper audit. A factory audit where your QA team visits the manufacturing facility will typically uncover more potential areas of concern, but in a lot of cases, it is impractical due to the number of suppliers. Possibly, your volumes are lower, so a virtual audit is more in line with your available resources. Either way, the formal audit is extremely helpful. You want to look at the supplier's processes—how robust and well documented are they? How well do they support operators to eliminate errors?

Next, check the supplier's certifications. One of the most common is the ISO certifications, which verify that the supplier has processes and (most importantly) is actually following those processes. That external validation is significant.

Then discuss your design and how it will affect the testing requirements. For example, when we make displays for handheld products, we know they will be dropped at some point. We design them to survive being dropped, which is a complete integration between us and our customer, because both ourselves and the client have to design the whole product around protecting the glass.

Over the course of this process, you'll also discover whether the new supplier is well aligned with you in terms of industry and volume. When you buy through a distributor several layers removed from the manufacturer, you can't expect as much responsiveness to your needs. If you call them about a defect, the customer service person is limited in the information they can access. They can see that you placed the order. They can replace the defective part. But they can't work with you on a corrective action process to stop those defects in the future. Suppliers will invest more effort into corrective actions, containment, and collaboration with their most significant customers. Therefore, it's in your best interest to be a significant client or realign yourself with a different supplier.

GREAT ALIGNMENT FOR A GREAT RELATIONSHIP

A significant customer of ours uses older display technology with a resistant touch panel that naturally has a lot of variation from one unit to the next. It's just part of the manufacturing process. Each part has to be calibrated before it can be used. So, for example, when the end user pushes on the red box, the signal registers an accurate location.

Our customer didn't have the capability to calibrate the touch panels as part of their product features, so we saw a lot of parts returned even though they were technically within specifications. Theoretically, we could have shrugged our shoulders and said, "Those parts are in spec. You change."

But if we did that, the unit would fail and be rejected when it was tested on their side and the redesign to incorporate the initial calibration feature would be a major change to the product. That's a lot of extra expense. The most efficient solution was to tighten the spec beyond the capability of the touch panel materials, do the mock calibration testing at our own facility, and eliminate any product that was outside of the customer's new, tighter specification. So we took on the responsibility to make sure those panels were within a tight enough tolerance to eliminate the need for calibration before we shipped them out.

The only way to test them properly was inside the customer's full assembly. We inserted ten of our customer's terminals into our production line, and part of the final test was to test every single display directly on our customer product. We created a practical use tolerance "go/no go" touch panel test that allowed us to eliminate the outliers that would not have actually performed well in the end product due to the product's limitations.

This kind of cooperation is one of the benefits of a great fit between customer and supplier. In a great customer-supplier relationship, you can expect complete flexibility in solving problems because it's all about delivering the most overall efficiency between the combined set of companies and creating the most value. Sometimes this means when there's a need, more work falls on the supplier that might be out of scope. And this is the correct answer when out-of-scope work can be done more efficiently (i.e., more cost effectively) by the supplier than if it was performed by the customer. The most efficient solution is not to minimize each partner's work and cost but to create the most efficiency overall.

It's not always possible to be a significant customer to every vendor—a hobbyist who builds five units a year isn't going to get corrective actions from a vendor. They just use the standard return process. If you're building ten thousand a year and your supplier is filling orders in the millions, you won't get the attention you deserve. But you might be a significant customer to someone else.

Now that you've vetted a new supplier on their quality and alignment, don't forget you also need to vet them on the other four supply chain problems. So let's move on to discuss how you can address issues with performance.

CHAPTER 5

===

PERFORMANCE

OBSOLESCENCE   DELIVERY   QUALITY   **PERFORMANCE**   COST   NEW PRODUCT DESIGN

I love wakeboarding, and I love this device I had on my boat from a company called PerfectPass. It precisely controls the boat's speed, which is incredibly necessary for skiing and watersports. This device was so good that it was nicknamed the "marriage saver" because it eliminated so many arguments when the rider would complain to their significant other driving the boat about the inconsistent speed. But I'm also a display guy, so I love displays—and although I loved the product, I didn't love the display on my PerfectPass unit. The device works great, but the display gave the product a dated look, and the colors clashed with their different branded designs.

So back in 2006 in the early days of my company, I cold-called PerfectPass and told them how I felt about the product (mostly good, because we all know nobody likes to hear that their baby is ugly). I suggested we could help them update it to have a better look and feel for the end users. They appreciated the feedback (especially the part where I told them how well it works), but they weren't overly interested in changing.

That's not surprising. Nobody wants to change—changing requires work! It's scary and expensive and comes with risk. They would have had to vet us and probably didn't know how. There's always a lot of resistance to doing something different. But we stayed in conversation for about a year. Over time, the people I was speaking with started to open dialogue inside their company about the idea of updating the design and display. The idea gained momentum, and eventually they sent us their design to see what we could do with it.

When we looked inside the unit, things started to get really interesting. These units had been in production for a while. When they were first designed, they used the most current display technology at the time. Since then, the industry had moved on, and I could see it was time to upgrade the glass type. Beyond that, there was an octopus of wires and connectors linking the display to the rest of the unit.

They'd originally designed the unit around a standard off-the-shelf display that came with a certain type of interface. They had to create an intermediary printed circuit board (PCB) with its own interconnect to mount to the display. Then that PCB had another interconnect to mount to the main product. There were a lot of extra parts in there.

Every single component on your bill of materials costs money to manage. They create extra steps in your manufacturing process. And they create potential points of quality failure, or opportunities for obsolescence or delivery hang-ups that can interrupt your production line. I knew we could do a lot to make this product perform better inside as well as outside. We would be able to make an improvement to cost, performance, and quality, as well as simplify their supply chain and reduce that intangible risk by improving the LCD glass technology and seamlessly integrating the internal components.

We designed a custom display for them with upgraded glass and integrated the daughter board directly into the display so that the new display would connect directly to their main PCB. We eliminated unnecessary components, simplified their supply chain, and increased their operational efficiency and overall performance. We gave them a product that cost less to build, that also looked better, and worked more reliably for the end user.

Before we started collaborating on the design, the clients didn't have a clear understanding of how much value an upgrade might add to their product. Upgrading a component usually means increasing costs for that part. Then there's market analysis that needs to be done to determine whether you'll be able to sell more products or sell the same product for more.

As it turned out, the performance upgrade to the new Perfect-Pass unit also came with a cost savings at the system level, so that was a win-win-win. The best part? They sent me one of the new units to replace the one on my boat. It looks fantastic, and I love telling the story every time I'm out on the water.

PERFORMANCE AND PROFIT

If you see two products that sell for the same price but one is better than the other, then there is no market for the lower-performing item. It will just cease to exist. Take the example of 1980s picture-tube TVs (CRT) compared to today's flat screens. There's just no market for CRTs anymore. The CRTs have a much lower resolution, they cannot be built as large, the contrast is far lower, they are so thick they need their own furniture to hold them up—and the killer is that they're more expensive. When it's this obvious, no market analysis is really required to understand it. We just go with the higher performance because it makes no sense to purchase an inferior product at a higher price.

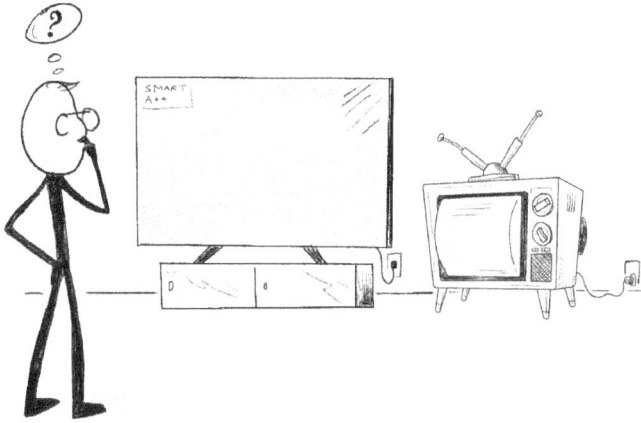

If there's a cost difference involved, the market forces get more complicated. Let's say you have a display in your product and you're considering increasing the brightness. The performance upgrade will cost 20 percent more, or three bucks per display.

How is that going to affect your profit per unit? If you can't sell your end product for more, or alternatively sell more units of your end product, then you haven't gained anything and you're just going to make less money. Nobody wants that. There would have to be a cost benefit on the other side of that equation for the performance enhancement to make financial sense. Again, we are all in business, so this boils down to simple economics every time. Will the financial benefit outweigh the cost of the performance improvement? If not, you don't do it. It's that simple.

One could argue, "Well, my product needs this to be able to function at the standard of my other products." Okay, I understand the motivation, but at the end of the day, if you cannot increase your profitability for this performance improvement, then your customers are not recognizing the value of it. That means you're choosing to subsidize that expense out of your own profits.

This is where your marketing and sales people come in to assess whether a brighter display will move more products or justify a price increase. Once you have those estimates, you make the call: is the upgrade worth it?

I'm not an expert in the individual industries of every single one of our clients; I'm a display expert. So if you ask me whether you should upgrade your performance, I'd have to ask you, will it make you more money?

Occasionally, a customer describes their product's usage to me, and I have to tell them that the performance specifications they want are just overkill. More performance doesn't always mean more value, and we'll go into that more deeply when we discuss cost in Chapter 6. I want to make sure that a customer's wish-list items are really in their best interest. Performance and profit are always related, and you need to make sure that curve is bending in the right direction.

IDENTIFYING PERFORMANCE ISSUES

Most of the time, you won't be in a situation like PerfectPass was with me, where I as the end user offered to redesign part of the product (or at least, not one who actually knows what they're doing). You have to be aware and proactive to identify when there are issues with your product's performance or you're lagging behind the market.

Customer feedback is usually the first place performance issues are identified. Dissatisfied customers are most likely to complain and will start with terms like "low quality" because, as we discussed in the last chapter, most people don't draw the distinction between quality and performance. If your company sees these complaints ticking up and you dismiss them, you are missing the opportunity. You could say that the product performs according to specifications, so the quality is just fine. That may be technically true, but unhappy customers don't stay customers for long. Your customers are hinting to you that your product needs to be designed to specifications that meet their expectations.

The second way to identify performance gaps is to look around your industry. What's your competition doing? Are you lagging behind? If your product has fewer features or performs to a lower specification, does your price advantage support the reduced product capability? (I'm assuming that in this case, there is a price advantage, otherwise you don't have a market for your product anyway.) Or are you the leader in your industry, and if so, what does that mean for your product's capabilities and your customer experience? Conversely, if you are charging a premium, do the additional features or performance justify this additional cost?

The worst-case scenario for performance would be that you're simply not meeting your market's needs for a product, and you're losing sales. If you're getting beat out of the market by your competitors, it's past time to start thinking about upgrading your performance. We can't all be Steve Jobs and figure out what customers want before they even want it. Most of us perform reactively. We change because of a pain point. If you're already sensing the pain of reduced sales forecasts, don't let it slide. You don't want your product to wind up on the scrap heap like the old CRT televisions.

Whether you're trying to catch up to your competitors or thinking outside of the box to get ahead of the curve, it's a good idea to open up a conversation with your current supplier about different ways a performance upgrade could help you in the marketplace. I'd encourage you to simply ask an open-ended question to your supplier: "How could you enhance my product?" If your supplier is ready to work on performance with you, their first response better be the question "Who is your customer and how are they using your product?" Then they can lead the discussion from there to explore different features that could benefit your end user.

YOUR SUPPLIER RELATIONSHIP

When you start conversations about performance upgrades with your supplier, you'll discover some vital information about the long-term viability of your relationship: Can they change with you? Are they willing to change with you?

In your personal life, a long-term relationship has to leave room for both partners to grow and change. Sometimes those changes enhance the partnership. Other times, they make it very challenging to continue. For example, if you met your significant other in college, maybe you both planned to focus on your careers and do a lot of traveling. You weren't interested in kids anytime soon, maybe never.

Five or six years later, you might think differently. You've been there, done that, traveled all over Europe and now you want to start a family. Does your partner want the same thing? Are they willing and able to go down that new life path with you?

Neither of you did anything wrong or let each other down in any way. But you have grown into a new set of needs. You have to figure out together whether this relationship can take you both where you want to go.

TRUST YOUR EXPERT

We're in a very complicated business. Nobody can be an expert in every aspect of their supply chain because there is so much variation and specialization in electronic components. One of the challenges for me in particular is that I'm always having conversations with clients about things they can't see—even though displays are all about what you can see!

We talk about how many pixels you have, the contrast ratio, and color gamut. We describe brightness with a seemingly arbitrary measure called a nit. Can you close your eyes and visualize the difference between 600 and 700 nits? To be honest, it is nearly impossible to tell the difference with your eyes open! There are a lot of very specific terms that I wouldn't expect a client to understand, and the same is going to be true about the exact technical specifications of many components you're buying.

You shouldn't have to walk into this conversation as a display expert with a list of precise specifications like "I need a contrast ratio greater than 900 to 1." Back it up. Instead, talk to your vendor about your product and your end user: what are you building, and how will your customers use it? What exactly do you need it to do? How does your user interact with the product? What environment or setting is it built for? And what does your user care about the most?

When my customers share this deep understanding of their product and their users' needs, I can translate that into technical specifications. That's my job. Not only should you be able to trust your supplier's expertise, but you need to lean on them to steer you into the best component possible for your end product.

SET EXPECTATIONS

In the same way that we discussed in early chapters, your relationship with your supplier depends largely on your alignment. Your volumes and your importance to them as a customer will govern how much flexibility and collaboration they will typically offer.

A hobbyist who buys a few units a year is going to find the best fit with a distributor who offers standard products off the shelf. Hopefully, the sales rep can give advice about which product is the best choice. But more often than not, that sales rep may be someone wearing a headset in a large call center, who may or may not really understand the wide scope of products they offer, let alone your specific performance needs. On the other end of the spectrum, Steve Jobs could just walk into a supplier's office, tell them what he wanted (even if it didn't exist yet), and they'd build it for him.

Your business is probably somewhere in the very, very large middle of that range. So talk to your supplier about your needs. Make sure to include what isn't working about your current configuration. What do you wish could be better? Don't constrain your wish list at the beginning. The supplier should be able to bring you back to reality if you start violating the laws of physics.

WHEN YOU REACH AN IMPASSE

Just like in a personal relationship, I always advocate talking to your partner first. Find out what options you have to continue moving forward together. Those options give you one data point. The challenge in relationships is, it's hard to know what to do with one data point.

Unlike a personal relationship, it's always okay to take this next step: talk to another supplier, and maybe a third, and comparison shop. Then you'll get to the best answer. Maybe you'll discover that you're already in an optimal situation with your current vendor. Maybe you'll discover that the thing you want doesn't exist, and you aren't quite hitting the volume to support having suppliers invent entirely new technologies for you. Or maybe you'll discover a vendor with the right alignment who can help you get your product where you want it to go.

VETTING FOR PERFORMANCE

When you interview these potential new vendors, you're going to start at the same place you started with your current supplier. Talk about your product, your users, your current challenges, and your goals. The discussions you already had with your supplier will probably help generate new questions to ask and uncover important details you can share.

SPECIAL PERFORMANCE FOR SPECIAL NEEDS

Your specific needs for your product drive your performance requirements, and it's especially important to share any special needs with a new vendor who isn't already familiar with your company. For example, we've designed displays for a product that's used in a very volatile environment with explosive gases all around. It required an LCD display module that is intrinsically safe, meaning that there could not be any exposed electrodes that could create any sort of spark whatsoever. That's a much more specific requirement than your average LCD display. This type of special need is going to be unique to your product and can be game changing for your supplier selection process.

One important consideration is how big an impact a particular component has on the user's experience. In my world, some products are what I call display-centric. These are products where the display experience is fundamental to the overall use of the product. This type of display-centric product would include cell phones, laptops, TVs, or wearables. Your smartphone, for instance, needs high-performance display-related components so that you can have an optimal experience watching movies or playing games. You probably interface with it almost entirely through the display. So in these products, the display needs to be very high performance in order to make the end product outperform the competition.

Non-display-centric products are those where the display is not as much of a key part of achieving a level of the end products' performance, but rather the display is only a means to communicate with the user. Don't get me wrong—as I need to stay in business—the display is still important, but there is a distinction where an improved display correlates much less to an improved end product. This group comprises the majority of electronics out there and includes handheld instrumentation like the explosive-gas detection meter or medical devices like a pulse oximeter. In both of these cases, the product performance is more related to the algorithms and sensors and less dependent on the size, resolution, and contrast of the display. The main function of the gas detection product is to detect gases. The readout is just there to show the numbers (and not explode).

Although we are more used to experiencing display-centric products in our everyday life, these non-display-centric electronics actually make up the majority of the products being manufactured. And this is why it's critical to understand the relationship between adding value to a component, like an LCD display, and the resulting added value to the end product—they don't always correlate.

Another great example of special-need products are the displays we create for snowmobiles. Now, snowmobiles operate in snow, and for snow to stay snow, it means the weather is very, very cold. So these units need to actually function down to –40°C.

The thing is, an LCD's main component that makes the magic

happen is in fact a *liquid*. And when this liquid gets colder, the molecules move slower and they become more and more viscid. The liquid crystal needs to move inside of the display, so this thickening and slowing cause the display to become harder to operate, meaning it requires a much higher voltage. And eventually, if you get this liquid cold enough, it will freeze. When you freeze a liquid crystal cell, the same thing happens as when you freeze a full bottle of water: it expands and bursts. The display glass will break, and it's all over.

Normally operating LCDs are designed to function at temperatures from 50°C down to 0°C. And the range for the extended-temperature LCD display is from 70°C to –20°C. Negative twenty is no problem—we do that all the time. Negative forty, however, is a challenge.

This is where the PhDs come in. They had to design a specific fluid—actually, a combination of different fluids—that could withstand that extreme cold but still operate at warmer temperatures (since the unit still has to survive summer, even when it's not being used). A fluid that moves well at cold temperatures is called fast. The thing is, a fluid that's fast enough to work in the cold when things really slow down is going to be too fast when temperatures are warmer. Too fast translates to a lower-contrast display, all the way down to an illegible display.

On the other hand, too slow of a fluid at the lower temperature can either take too long to update the LCD image, or it will not be able to update at all. These designs are complicated. It's a fine balance between using the ideal temperature compensation with the right LCD fluid. And sometimes even that isn't enough, so we add a heater to either the front or the rear of the display to meet the extreme conditions. This example isn't like your iPhone where the critical attributes of the display are size, resolution, contrast, and viewing angle for the ideal experience. For products like the snowmobiles, the critical attribute is to be able to operate in a very extreme environmental condition and simply indicate a few critical functions.

Whether your product needs to be frozen in the Arctic, go to the bottom of the ocean, avoid static discharge, work in direct sunlight, be intrinsically safe, be low power, the list goes on—there are a lot of technical specifications that must be precisely adjusted for extreme performance conditions. All those requirements are vital for a potential vendor to know so they can collaborate with you effectively.

CAN THEY? WILL THEY?

Now that you've explored the scope of your needs with a new vendor, it's time to talk about what they can do to accommodate you. Since your existing part was either designed specifically for you or you have designed specifically around it, any change to that one part will most likely affect many other components. Does this new supplier already have an available product that will drop right into your design, or are they willing to match and customize one to bring it in line with your needs? Are they willing to do that for your specific type of product and for your anticipated annual mass production volumes?

Since you're looking at the possibility of replacing an existing part in your product configuration, you have to discuss the issue of compatibility. What will it take to make the new vendor's part work seamlessly with your product? Getting as close as possible to seamless transition and integration is critical. You don't want to wind up with an octopus of interconnections and accommodations because of a new vendor's standard parts. That's just going to create more hassle, expense, and future opportunities for failure.

Will your supplier take responsibility for the design of the new part? This is especially pertinent when you're dealing with so many different attributes (as we do). For example, an LCD display has mechanical requirements, electrical requirements, optical requirements, and even requires some minor software updates when looking to match an existing component. We have done this for so many successful projects and it is so essential to obtain the desired results that we developed our own Cross-Match Process. (We'll discuss that further in Chapter 8.) It's important to understand the boundaries of what your supplier can and can't do.

If you're a lower-volume customer, you might be confined to a vendor's standard product range, as the customization usually comes with minimum volume constraints. This is a much tougher process, and it's a matter of finding the closest alternative to the component that you are replacing, while still resolving all of the five problems with this component. If you're purchasing higher volumes, you should have more options available for customization. Alignment with your vendor matters just as much for performance issues as for every other supply chain issue.

VETTING COMPREHENSIVELY

Remember, vetting a new supplier on any one of the five problems must always lead back to vetting them on the other four as well. Upgrading your performance with the right supplier should give you improvements or risk reduction in all five areas, not just in performance alone.

Components that are more common with current industry standards will have a longer life span before they go obsolete. A simpler design and good integration reduce the number of subcomponents you're using and save you on costs at both the part and manufacturing levels. Setting your performance standards at the right level for your product's usage can save on costs, too.

Costs aren't the first issue that will prompt a change of supplier, but they are critical and they go right to the bottom line. We'll talk about them next.

CHAPTER 6

COST

OBSOLESCENCE   DELIVERY   QUALITY   PERFORMANCE   **COST**   NEW PRODUCT DESIGN

Cost is actually the last reason a manufacturer thinks about change. This may be surprising to most, but when you think about it, it's the smallest change agent out of the five problems. **Obsolescence** is shutting down your entire production if not resolved. **Delivery** is costing you clients, affecting your manpower efficiencies and causing a lot of catch-up expedites. **Quality** has high costs in loss of clients, rework, and possibly product recalls. **Performance**, if overdesigned, will include waste in every single product or, if underdesigned, will not be as competitive in the market and result in lower sales. Then there's **cost** where if you're not aligned correctly, you could be paying up to 20 percent over the most efficient market price for your component.

But in most cases, that 20 percent delta is far less than the costs that result from the other four problems. At the time of writing this book, it's 2021 and we are in the middle of a global chip (IC) shortage, which I would put in the delivery category of problems. I have had so many conversations with so many customers that ended with "I would gladly pay double if I could get the product today." This example hammers home that delivery is so much more important than cost.

Don't get me wrong, cost is still important. It may be last on the list, but it's still on the list.

Recently, we were approached by a client looking for a cost reduction. Their product is an alarm and communication system for public and industrial buildings. It has a larger LCD display that can either show a time-date clock (when there is no alarm in progress) or a warning with additional information, like the nearest exit route.

The customer was paying a lot for these displays, and since a display is typically one of the highest cost items on any bill of materials, the client started their cost-reduction initiative to increase profitability and marketability by bringing their costs down.

As soon as we saw their design, it was clear that their display was completely overdesigned for the application. The display specifications called for a super-high resolution, very bright outdoor display backlighting that just didn't make any sense. We knew we could do better for them.

The content they were showing was very, very simple. They

needed to display large, bold letters that were visible from far away. High resolution is important when you are re-creating photographs or people's faces. It doesn't do anything for a simple coarse alphanumeric signboard. They'd also specified extreme brightness that would be appropriate for an outdoor situation in harsh sunlight. But this was an indoor product.

Any attribute or feature in a product that doesn't add value for the customer is waste, so all that excess performance was overkill. They were paying for things that did not bring value to the end customer. In fact, the display was so bright that it had to be turned down below 50 percent of its brightness for its end use application.

How or why did this happen? The customer wasn't dumb. They started with the size of their product, which dictated a certain size of wide-format display. At the time they started developing the product, the only standard product that they found that met their most critical first need (size) was this overdesigned component that had excess performance for their application. It was the only standard product available at the time, so they designed around what they could get.

By the time they came to us, their product had been in production for three years, and another option had become available in the market. We had access to a much simpler glass design. We could dispense with the high resolution because you couldn't even see the difference in their content. We also redesigned the backlight to be appropriate for a high-end indoor application. By cutting out all of this unnecessary resolution and brightness, we were able to bring down their display costs by about 40 percent.

COST AND PROFITABILITY

The cost of your product is more than the sum of the components and labor that go into it. There's the burden—the indirect infrastructure supporting the labor and material management. The burden cost of components typically ranges from 20 to 30 percent, so for every dollar in increased cost of parts or labor, the total increase to the organization is about $1.20 to $1.30.

When you follow your product all the way through your distribution and sales channel to your end customer, you're often looking at an end customer price of two to five times the material costs, depending on your product and your market.

So every dollar you spend on a component pushes up your end price, and every dollar you save could potentially reduce your product price by up to five dollars. That flexibility creates more market opportunity, while overpaying for components will make your product less marketable. Or since something has to give, it will make you less profitable.

Cost is critical to your long-term profitability because the cost of a single component is multiplied through your manufacturing and sales chain. These costs have an exponential impact on your customers. But there's more to the story: even when manufacturers know cost is a problem, it's not usually the first problem they're looking to solve.

THE LAST PROBLEM

Back in Chapter 1, I mentioned Mary, the buyer I offered 30 percent savings to. At the time, I didn't understand that cost is the very last reason most manufacturers think about changing vendors. There's a very good reason for that: the other four problems cost far more than you could typically save on a single component!

Is saving 20 or 30 percent on one part really worth it if you have to manage a new risk of obsolescence or delivery failures? I've heard many clients say they'd happily pay double if I could deliver a part when their regular supplier let them down. The same holds true for quality and performance—how much will you spend on field returns if the quality doesn't hold up? How much business would you lose if the performance doesn't represent your product well?

On top of that, the pain of changing suppliers isn't just a pain in the neck. It's a pain in the bottom line. The process of identifying, qualifying, and integrating a new part into your product takes time and money. All in all, I list cost as the fifth of five problems because the pain of the other four problems is greater to an organization, but cost is still a critical pain point and is one of the areas you must manage in order to maximize your business.

THE FIRST QUESTION

Oddly enough, when a potential customer reaches out to me, cost is the first thing they want to talk about. Every discussion starts with defining the product just enough to open the discussions about cost. That's why in my earlier years I used to give cost the pole position in the list of the five problems.

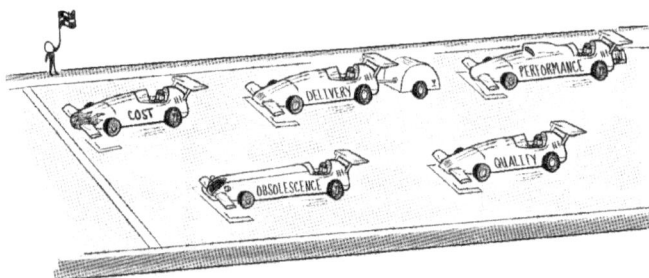

It took me some time to retrain my brain. When speaking with potential clients, I'm always careful about how I present this stance. If a supplier says, "Cost isn't important" to you, you expect that you are going to be getting out your wallet. It's easily misinterpreted as a sales tactic for very expensive suppliers to push their features and try to justify their higher cost. That's because we see this line used manipulatively in our everyday consumer life. We know when we are at the Ferrari car dealership, we are not getting the most economically efficient method of transportation.

Here's the difference: cost does matter, but you can't make a final decision based on cost *alone*. It is the full combination of solving and optimizing all five problems which lead to the most cost-effective solution at a system level. Cost alone can be a misleading indicator when it doesn't factor in the effects from the other four problems—rework and returns, missed commitments and lost sales, redesign and delays due to obsolescence, and underperforming your market.

The other reason cost comes first on the conversation list is that it's the easiest to talk about. There's a discrete dollar amount tied to this metric, and it makes it simple to compare one supplier to another. Comparing vendors across any of the other problems is much more complicated. Obsolescence requires knowing that the components you're offered have an appropriate life span and that your supplier is willing to support an obsolescence mitigation plan. Screening that level of detail from multiple suppliers can end up looking like a bunch of confusing sales pitches without much meaning behind them. The same goes for quality, delivery, and performance. Even though cost isn't the number one pain point in the supply chain world, it is a useful starting point. Cost is driven by alignment in several dimensions and allows you to quickly eliminate misaligned suppliers so you can focus on detailed vetting of the more complex problems with the remaining few suppliers on your short list.

THE DRIVERS OF COST

Several factors influence the cost of your components:

- Features
- Performance

- Quality
- Volume
- Distribution channel

Each of these elements need to be properly aligned to your market, industry, and end users. If you're out of alignment on the low end, you'll wind up with problems in performance, quality failures, or order fulfillment. When you're out of alignment in the other direction, you wind up paying more than you should. Let's look at each one.

FEATURES

In our example of the ski boat system in Chapter 5, there were additional components on our display to help integrate it to the customer's product, like an additional PCB and a connector. Including those components made more sense for the customer based on economics, quality, and ease of manufacturing analyses. Although the price per unit for the displays did go up, the overall system-level cost of the end product went down.

Similarly, adding a feature will raise the cost. Touch panels, buttons, LED indicators, and custom overlays are some of the most common feature sets that are included. There are two simple questions to guide you in making the right decisions about additional features. First, will this added feature increase the value to the customer in excess of its cost? Second, is it more cost efficient to have this feature included on the display or to purchase it separately and assemble it yourself?

PERFORMANCE

As we saw in the example of our alarm system customer, it doesn't make sense to pay for higher performing attributes that add no value for your end user. In this example, both the pixel resolution and the brightness were far in excess of what the end customer ultimately valued. Valuable performance creates more profit by allowing you to raise your prices or sell more products. Nonvalued performance, on the other hand, simply creates waste. A good value isn't necessarily low cost—it aligns your product's features and components with the needs of your end user so that the price you pay translates into value to the end customer and ultimately profit.

QUALITY

As we discussed in Chapter 4, the quality of your components needs to be aligned with your industry standards. If you're using consumer-grade components for an industrial application, you'll get more failures and returns because they won't hold up to the typical rigors of industrial use.

Be careful because on paper, you will see a cost benefit because you're purchasing a lower cost (and lower quality) product. Once in production, your cost of quality will show up in your bottom line through more out-of-the-box failures, assembly line failures, and field failures. In the end, any apparent savings per component will not only be negated over time, but you wind up paying more at an overall system level for lower quality.

By the same token, paying for components that were designed to a much higher standard than you need (like aerospace) is also going to wind up wasting money. In this case, let's assume you are building an industrial-type product like a kiosk. The difference in quality between an industrial-grade component and an aerospace-grade component doesn't add enough value to your kiosk to justify the huge difference in cost. The additional piece price becomes so high that it eats into your profit margin or worse, prices you out of the market altogether. Quality alignment produces optimal value.

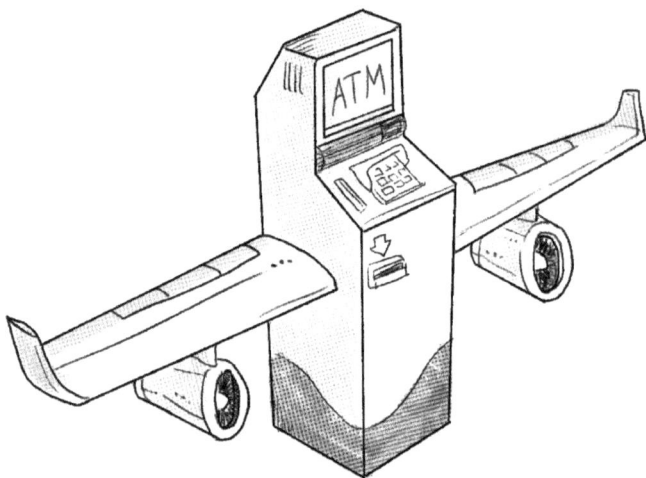

VOLUME

Sixteen years ago, we obtained our very first customer, a manufacturer of satellite phones. Their current vendor was an LCD display supplier that focused heavily on cell phone displays. Since this product falls into the handset category, it was a natural fit for them, despite their mid-tier volume levels. This client had a mature product and was running a cost-reduction initiative across all components to improve their profitability. The challenge for them was that they had a very complicated custom display and required that the replacement create absolutely no changes to their existing product or manufacturing process. Because their design was already mature, the engineering resources would not be available. The costs of change at this time would quickly outweigh any component-level cost savings.

We applied our cross-match program (which we'll discuss more in Chapter 8) and designed a replacement display that would integrate perfectly with their existing product. The biggest change we were able to make wasn't in the display at all—it was us. Their order sizes were aligned with our optimal volumes, and we were in the right industry to serve their needs. Our factory was right-sized for them, and so we were able to save them about 30 percent on their displays.

With their former supplier, the industry was a good match between the customer and the supplier, but the volumes were not. Cell phones run in the millions per year whereas this type of industrial product would fall into the category of tens of thousands. Quick math exposes a 100X delta in volume between the two customer types. Which one do you think they really cared about?

Volume matching is very important for controlling your costs. You have to work with the right size factories. For example, a hobbyist who needs to fabricate a prototype can't use the same supply chain as Ford Motors, who purchase with a million-dollar minimum order. And the converse is also true—Ford isn't going to work with a really small factory that has limited capacity because they can't hit the most efficient high-volume pricing. We build on an efficient assembly line so that we can deliver the lowest cost product to our customers, but that comes with minimum order quantities. MOQs could be as low as 500 units or as high as 5,000 or more.

You need to find your level. If your product is lower volume, but conversely the supplier you work with is set up for higher volumes, there are two effects. First, the setup costs are much higher for each manufacturing run. Higher volume setups are far more complex. In order to optimize efficiency at scale, the manufacturer uses more automation, tooling, fixtures, and infrastructure. That complexity makes the initial setup more expensive but saves money per unit at high volume.

But for a lower volume project, this oversized setup fee (amortized across the production run) will increase the per-unit costs of the component. In the example of our satellite phone customer, their manufacturing runs were 100 times smaller than the supplier's average customer. The supplier would apply their internal setup fee each time they manufactured this display, which made the setup cost more expensive per part by orders of magnitude.

The second effect was the impact on the supplier relationship. Customers need to be important to a supplier, just like the supplier is important to you because you need their components to build your product. We call this co-significance. If you are working with a supplier where your volumes are significantly lower than their typical client, then that supplier has to make up that significance gap somehow. That's typically done by charging a much higher margin on your lower volume project. And without that higher margin, the significance gap would become too large, and not only would this supplier not care about losing you as a client, they may actually want to lose you as a client.

You can easily imagine the quality of a relationship that only one party wants to be in!

Now, if your project is higher volume than your supplier's typical client base, then you have a different set of alignment issues. First, your lower volume supplier will have a less complex setup and lower setup fees, but the reduced operational efficiency during the actual production run would increase the unit price. Second, you may run into capacity issues. If your volumes are significantly larger, they may strain the supplier's systems and slow down production. Although this isn't directly related to your unit cost, it will impact your supply chain by creating delivery issues if the supplier's factory can't keep up.

DISTRIBUTION CHANNEL

Volume also impacts how the product gets to you. A product might be built in high volume but sold in smaller quantities through several layers of distribution. Big-name displays like Sharp, NEC, and Samsung are great examples of that. They're manufactured in very large quantities, but if you need to buy only five or ten units, you'll wind up paying a lot more per unit to a small distributor. Every layer of distribution that touches your component increases the cost. The right supplier for the inventor is completely different from the right fit for Ford, but they're both out there. Your right fit is out there, too. The rule of thumb is to work as close to the manufacturer as your volumes permit. Distributors add value, but they also add cost and complexity in communication.

YOUR SUPPLIER RELATIONSHIP

When I think of cost burdens in the context of a personal relationship, I'd describe it as negative energy. There are all kinds of ways that two people can create friction with each other, and it all adds up. When the burden of that negative energy gets too high in a personal relationship, it shows up as resentment, and in the case of this commercial relationship, it shows up as increased system-level costs. In both cases, it is not easy to measure and quantify. But if you are sensing the friction, you need to address it.

The important thing to consider is whether the problem is the other person, the situation, or you. If you're the source of the negative energy, you won't find the solution by simply changing partners.

The same holds true for your supplier relationship. Are they really the source of the cost problem? If your specifications are off, your assembly is too challenging to build without defects, or your manufacturing systems are not adequately supporting your product, then changing suppliers will only create more damage and cost to you.

I've even seen customers shoot themselves in the foot with internal cultural issues that blow up their costs. For example, a client of ours makes a highly specialized type of gauge panel. They're a huge corporation with many different divisions. Unfortunately, the different groups that we have to work with are all siloed from one another, and there's no internal cooperation at all.

Every action and project is urgent. Of course, in practice that means nothing is urgent, and nothing can actually be prioritized over something else if they are all living at the same urgency. The engineering department will demand high resolution without regard to price, and when the order goes through purchasing, they won't accept it due to the higher costs. Designs will get pushed through without consulting Quality Assurance, so then QA comes in at the last minute requesting major changes and additional quality testing. We've often wound up trying to referee disputes between different groups in their organization.

Everything is high stress, everything is expedited, and everything goes through more revisions and iterations than it should. As a result, the process takes longer and costs more for a lower quality result. Some organizations believe that pushing their suppliers as hard as they can will result in better value. In reality, the best value comes from a partnership—just like your personal relationships.

A great vendor wants to work with you for eight, ten, fifteen years—for the life of your product—and keep you for the next product after that. They aren't looking to overcharge you or cut corners. The best way you can control your costs is to invest in the value of your supplier relationship.

To work with your current supplier on managing costs, you need to consider the overall environment, validate your costs by comparing quotes, and consider the potential for system-level savings. Again, just like your personal relationships, you need to look at yourself first.

ENVIRONMENTAL FACTORS

At the time of this writing, we're in the middle of the 2021 electronic component pandemic. Across the board, lead times for all electronics are moving out further and further and have actually spread throughout the economy to affect just about every commodity manufactured. We're seeing six- to twelve-month lead times on our specialty LCD driver ICs. Shipping is expensive. Labor is expensive. Everything is expensive.

Fortunately, our customers are aware of the situation—you can hardly miss it. In normal times, you still need to be aware of the overall environment. If your supplier is notifying you of cost increases, look around. Is this happening just to you, or is it happening to everyone? Is this increase due to the supplier's choices, or are they dealing with larger market forces beyond their control?

COMPARE QUOTES

As a manufacturer and sales organization, I don't love to give my clients this advice, but it's good advice: when you're faced with a price increase, do some comparison shopping.

This step puts the control back into your hands. From my perspective, the worst thing would be for me to push through a price increase, have my customer do their research, and discover that some of my competitors don't have the same constraints I do and aren't raising their prices the same way. That would put my overall business at risk, and I never want to lose an aligned customer. It's a hundred times harder to find a new customer than to keep an existing one! That's why we work so hard to investigate and contain cost increases for our current clients.

When we're sourcing components, we start with the same process

I'm recommending to you. We start evaluating a subcomponent to determine if there is any waste by checking whether we're paying for anything we don't really need. We make sure our suppliers (and their subsuppliers) are aligned on volume levels. We challenge the cost internally and externally. We validate cost increases with other suppliers. We look at alternative subcomponents and different purchasing quantities to maximize value and keep our prices the same for our customers if possible.

To have a great long-term relationship with your supplier, ideally they would do the work up front to avoid cost increases whenever they can. That way, they'll never have to worry about you validating an increase against other suppliers' prices. But that's not always the case, and occasionally, that burden will fall on you.

MANAGING SYSTEM-LEVEL COSTS

When you're controlling costs, you need to consider both the unit price of a component and its system-level cost. Your costs at the system level represent the true cost impact of a component, far more than just the price shown on my purchase order.

Earlier, we looked at the ways quality can impact the overall cost to your business, because lower quality components require more management and experience more returns. There are a number of opportunities to lower your overall costs by paying a slightly higher unit price.

For example, a higher-end connector might be easier for your operators to assemble, which can lower the management burden and reduce assembly time. Precision materials can enable additional manufacturing efficiency. Saving minutes on the assembly line can be well worth the tens of cents you might invest in upgrading a component.

Another inflection point for reducing system-level cost is the placement of features. Your supplier may be able to save you a significant amount by doing more of the assembly work for you.

Some of the subcomponents that you source and assemble into your product might be obtained and placed more efficiently by your supplier in their facility. We build our displays in clean rooms in Asia with a very efficient assembly labor cost structure, while most of our customers build domestically. Our labor costs are much lower and we're able to add components at a much lower cost.

Sometimes a customer will add a touch panel to their display on their own assembly line. In 99.9 percent of cases, we'll be able to place that panel cheaper and better. Because we procure touch panels at higher overall volumes and we have expertise on that particular component, we can source and manage the panels better. Additionally, we can do the whole process in the same clean room as the LCD display assembly. In this example, if you have a clean display and a clean touch panel, it would decrease your manufacturing efficiency to take them out of that controlled environment, ship them, and then re-create the clean conditions for assembly. Producing the items together also eliminates the management cost of an additional component.

Another scenario where placement matters would be adding gaskets that fit between the display and the rest of your product. You receive the part ready to drop into your product, without additional handling or preassembly. Connectors, cables, indicator lights, brackets, switches, or even additional ICs—the list goes on and on—can all be manufactured in our facility and become part of the LCD display assembly.

Naturally, these additions increase the unit price of a display. But they can create a great deal of efficiency in your manufacturing process and thereby improve your system-level costs, reducing the end products' overall manufacturing costs.

VETTING ON COST

If you aren't satisfied with your current supplier's cost management and comparing quotes indicates that you might be able to find better value elsewhere, you need to vet the alternate supplier thoroughly. Assess them for alignment on volume, distribution, quality, and system-level efficiencies.

Make sure your product definition is very clear so you can get an accurate quote. Take into account whether the supplier is quoting the part exactly as you specify, or if they have exceptions. And consider how those exceptions might impact the rest of your product or your process. Exceptions are not always a bad thing. We also operate a custom cable assembly business and one of the main added-value services we offer is sourcing compatible alternate connectors at a much lower cost than the name-brand equivalents. However, in the first round of comparing quotes, I'd advise you to stick to the specifications—meaning no alternate components—so you can compare apples to apples. Then you can dig deeper.

Think about the volumes you need and ask about their typical client volumes. Ask about their minimum order quantities so you can get the most out of volume discounts. Consider your purchasing patterns and how you will take the product: is it yearly, quarterly, monthly, or even weekly? If you aren't buying directly from the manufacturer, find out how many layers are in the distribution chain and whether they all add value, because each layer adds to your cost.

When you're looking for new ways to create high-level efficiencies, it makes sense to consider customization. The right supplier can tailor a component for you to create massive value for your organization.

THE VALUE OF CUSTOMIZATION

There's a common misconception that custom items are always more expensive. That's what we're used to with consumer products. After all, if you want a custom-made dress shirt, it will cost $150, where you might pay $75 for ready-to-wear. A new iPhone is priced around a thousand bucks, while a custom, solid-gold and diamond smartphone could cost millions.

That's not always the case with this level of some of your indus-trial components—as long as you're matched with the right supplier. Now, for that hobbyist buying five components a year, it doesn't make sense. With low volumes like that, not only would it be impossible to get a supplier to create a custom solu-tion for you, but you'll be better off buying standard parts. But for ten thousand parts a year? At that volume, a customized solution can actually save you money.

Here's how it works. For a standard specialty component, the manufacturer already has everything tooled up for that con-figuration. The standard part "exists" in the sense that the manufacturer is ready to make it. They have samples and demos available, but they usually don't have an extra thousand units just sitting around on the shelves unclaimed and ready to ship. They have to go build those units to fill your order.

For a custom component (or a semi-custom component, which is more often the case, where we make a slight modification to an existing standard product), there's some work and cost up front for design and tooling. But once a component goes into production, there's typically no longer a cost difference between standard and custom parts. Once the tooling is complete and the new configuration exists, you can order standard or custom products the same way.

As for those upfront tooling costs, they can vary widely depend-ing on whether the individual subcomponents are fully custom or based on existing standards. Let's take a color display as an example. If your display needed a unique piece of TFT glass, that could push the tooling costs as high as $150,000. That wouldn't make any sense for most customers. But most of the time, an expense like custom glass is completely unnecessary. There are so many standard sizes of glass out there that nearly any product can be built around one. Tooling for a semi-custom display based on standard glass would cost somewhere between $2,000 and $7,000.

When we design custom parts, we have the opportunity to eliminate waste and get the appropriate interface. You may fall in between two standard sizes and need an additional mount, while a custom build can right-size the component to fit perfectly (for displays, that can add a lot of visibility and appeal for the end user). Similarly, you might be buying a standard component that's overdesigned for your needs, which is a waste of performance. Custom designs enable the component to fit your end product.

Customization can also improve your manufacturing process. I like to visit our customers' facilities to walk through the assembly line and talk to their operators. They're the ones who really know how easy and efficient it is to put our parts into the product, and they often have great ideas about how we could make it easier. Maybe a bolt is hard to screw in because it's set too close to another. Maybe a connector needs to be a little bit longer to plug in easily due to the complexity of the assembly process. If a small modification saves the operator a few seconds, over ten thousand times a year, that's going to create a big impact on your assembly costs.

So the question is, what benefit do you get from a custom component? You might gain performance and eliminate waste. It might improve your manufacturability. A $5,000 investment to get a custom part could end up saving $40,000 a month in system-level costs. Custom components aren't a luxury item. They can deliver great value. Most of our industrial customers have been building the same product for well over ten years. Ten years of production at the correct cost level improves the bottom line every time.

THE VALUE OF THE RIGHT SUPPLIER

When your prospective supplier checks out on cost, as always, don't stop there. You still need to vet them on all the other four problems. Those cost savings won't do you any good if they're masking an even riskier supply chain problem.

Finding a supplier who can work with you to reduce costs and add value makes a huge difference to your long-term profitability. They can reduce waste by removing features and functions that don't serve your end customer. They can offer volume discounts to align with your purchasing cycle. They can better integrate their parts into your product to make your manufacturing more efficient and your product more reliable. As a result of all these efficiencies, the overall cost of your product usually comes down, making your product more competitive and improving your profit margins.

So far, we've focused on solving problems. Now it's time to look ahead at new opportunities!

CHAPTER 7

NEW PRODUCT DESIGN

OBSOLESCENCE   DELIVERY   QUALITY   PERFORMANCE   COST   NEW PRODUCT DESIGN

One of the more unique experiences we've had in this business was working with the Santa Fe Opera. They were the first (and only) customer we've ever had that didn't produce a physical product. Instead, they were, as the name suggests, an opera house that needed our help restoring an important piece of infrastructure in their performance space.

The opera performs in a beautiful outdoor facility. The acoustics and the whole complex are amazing. One of the ways they make the performances more accessible and enjoyable for the audience is through their electronic libretto system—small displays in the back of each seat that display a translation of the lyrics into English or Spanish to help patrons follow the story.

The original system used vacuum fluorescent displays (VFDs), the type of segmented character display you used to see in digital clocks or car radios. VFD is a fifty-year-old technology that became common in the 1980s. It was very far out of date, and the exact displays the system required became obsolete years ago.

Over time, the displays failed, and the opera company could no longer find replacements. Their solution was to move the working displays forward so that the libretto translation became a perk for the expensive seats, but the cheaper seats and standing-room areas didn't have the option. They didn't love that solution because the whole point of the ELS was to make the opera more accessible to everyone!

They contacted us to inquire about designing a completely new LCD display that could work with the existing computer system. The challenge for us here was to *really* be the display experts because our customers didn't specialize in electronic design and manufacturing at all—they specialized in opera.

We started with the form factor because the chairs, brackets, and connections were already in place. We needed to create the closest possible match for their interface to minimize the financial impact on their system. Beyond that, we had to ensure the new displays would be robust enough to stay outdoors year-round and still have a long life span. The original system had been in place for decades, and the company certainly didn't want to replace it again anytime soon.

It was a unique project because it combined aspects of cross-matching to an existing system, with the requirement to design a completely new product instead of replicating the old one. We had to take the lead and guide the customer in choosing the right specifications. They were the experts in the experience they wanted to give their patrons, but they had to completely rely on our recommendations to bring that experience to reality.

The result was a new system that made us both proud—a high-resolution, full-color display that allows them to represent language translations clearly and accurately, as well as program more flexible messaging whenever they need to. The launch of the new system was so successful that other opera houses are looking to replicate it.

With all the challenges inherent in designing a new product from scratch, you also have a big advantage—you aren't trying to fix a failing relationship. You're making a fresh start. When you choose a supplier for your new product, don't just look for someone to take your order and fulfill it. Look for a partner who can collaborate with you and really invest in the success of your product.

YOUR TRUSTED ADVISOR

The team at the Santa Fe Opera leaned on our product knowledge because they had minimal experience building electronics. Even with our customers who build physical products, few clients are well versed in the details of our specific LCD niche in the industry. That's exactly as it should be! You are the expert in your end product, and you should be able to trust your component supplier to be the expert in their own field.

I was once invited to a meeting at the restaurant of a country club. The waiter asked me if I was ready to order, and I told him, "I haven't seen a menu yet."

He replied, "You don't need a menu here. You can have anything you want."

For about one second, I thought that sounded great. The next second, I realized I had no idea what to ask for. I'm not an expert chef, and I don't have a great imagination. I wound up eating a really boring sandwich and wishing I could have chosen from a list of amazing signature dishes.

I needed someone to give me advice so I could really take advantage of that opportunity. The same is true when you're designing a new product—you need someone who can take your goals for the end product and your knowledge of your end customer and translate them into specifications for their component. By bringing their expertise to meet your expertise, the right supplier can actually improve your design process. Lean on each other's knowledge, and you'll achieve the best result.

Now, there are technical discussions and there are marketing discussions. Your supplier can't tell you what your customer wants. You have to be the expert on that. They can't tell you whether a 3.5-inch or a 4.5-inch display would be better in your product. But they can tell you the costs and the performance impacts on the rest of your product design so you can make an informed product marketing decision.

To go back to the restaurant analogy, the waiter could tell you the specials of the day, but even the most helpful waiter can't tell you what you like to eat. They can't tell whether you're a vegetarian, or if you're allergic to onions. If you're in the mood for pasta, the expert can recommend a sauce. If you like steak, they could recommend some sides or a wine pairing. Still, you have to be the expert in your own needs, preferences, and goals.

With your product design, you have to be the expert in your end customer. How will they use the product? What sort of environment will they be in? What content will they need to have on the display, or how will they interact with a touch panel? Then your trusted advisor can guide you to the right component options.

BUILDING YOUR SUPPLIER RELATIONSHIP

When you thoroughly understand your customer and your product, it's time to start talking to suppliers. You don't need to have all the component specs determined before you start discovering what options are out there for you. I recommend talking to several different vendors to figure out how they are steering you toward the right technology that is going to serve your end customers the best. From there, you can begin to determine which ones have the best offer and the best process to work with you.

I know that can be an uncomfortable situation. I'm an engineer, and I talk to a lot of engineers. I hate picking up the phone without knowing every detail of what I'm talking about. That's okay. It's research. Don't start with super-technical details. The perfect place to start is, "I have a new product. Here's how it's intended to be used. What do you think might work well for this application?" A twenty-minute conversation early on can save you so much effort. It actually moves you ahead in your design process and is well worth the time.

The next question I always get after a technical discussion is about costs. That's important because you need to know if you're looking at a part that costs $150, $25, or $5. You might encounter an answer I've really learned to hate: "It depends."

That is such a useless answer. Of course it depends. Everything in this world depends on something! A good partner won't stop there. You need to paint a scenario together and see where it leads you, and that's what a helpful advisor can do for you. They can lead off with some assumptions they need to make to test out different parameters: if you need color, if you need a certain size and resolution. Then they can give a ballpark price and see if that might work for your project. You might respond with more detail about the environment or special performance needs. That's great! Now you can find a path to the best solution.

Every component has a variety of attributes. Start by establishing the biggest or most prominent and work your way down. For displays, that would mean starting with the size. Then you decide the technology type, color or monochrome. Then you can dive into different resolution options. Which attributes are most significant will vary by the type of component you're researching, but the pattern of largest to smallest is helpful for all of them. Again, the specifications for each attribute will be driven by what your product does, who your end user is, and how they're using it.

You'll also need to discuss your experiences and goals with the design process itself. What other products have you built, and what suppliers did you work with? What did you like or dislike about those products, and where do you see opportunities for improvement? Is there anything you'd like to improve in your own manufacturing process? Your supplier may be able to help optimize your operations by optimizing the design, as we discussed in Chapter 6.

I always advise people not to get wrapped up in the exact specifications up front. It's hard to understand what brightness or contrast mean in layman's terms. The description on paper doesn't necessarily convey the experience of seeing or interacting with the product in real life. You want your supplier to understand your purpose and help you design the best product for your application and not fall back on saying, "Well, this is the specification we agreed to."

At the end of the day, the specifications are just numbers. They are secondary. Serving your end users' needs is what matters. You need your supplier to help you find the component that really works in your product and then help you develop that specification around the end product's performance, not the other way around. You need a partner who supports your goals and creates these specs around your goals.

DESIGN FOR LONGEVITY

As you move forward exploring and selecting specific components, your supplier should be thinking ahead about your product's longevity. The more experience they have in your specific field and with your type of products, the more aware they'll be of industry trends and new options that might be available in six months or a year. They'll also have a better sense of what subcomponents are likely to disappear during the life span of your product. Obsolescence is one of the major risks you face with industrial products, so the right supplier will help you design for obsolescence mitigation.

An example that comes up in my niche is transflective TFT displays. Customers often want to use them for sunlight readability, and they work really well in those conditions. The problem is, transflective TFTs are a very unique, very hard-to-build product. When they go obsolete—and different configurations are going obsolete all the time—there aren't many options to replace them. The aggregate volumes for these types of TFT panels are often pretty low, so when a significant customer transitions out of this design, it often becomes unavailable to the rest of the market.

If a customer needs to use a product like this, we have to look very carefully at how long the glass might be available and compare it to the life span of the customer's product. We have to discuss whether the customer is prepared to do a last-time buy within two years or so because it's a real possibility. We'd usually recommend that they use a more common alternative component. In this case, that would be a standard transmissive display, with surface treatments and enhanced backlights to make it sunlight readable instead of truly transflective.

You run into a similar situation when a client is interested in using a very unique size or resolution of color TFT glass. We recommend against that for a couple of reasons. First, there are so many standard sizes and resolutions available that with some accommodation, we can find a more common platform that will still work well in the end product. With standard sizing, obsolescence is less likely, and we will have a lot more like-kind replacement options if the first production glass option goes obsolete. We can then switch to a replacement with minimal to no disruption to the customer. The second reason is that global volumes on standard-size glass are far higher, so the cost is typically lower.

The availability of your subcomponents will also affect the way a supplier builds their parts for you. Like 95 percent of all LCD displays, we manufacture our displays in China, and sometimes a customer will specify a US connector to put on our display. In practice, that connector is usually built in China and imported to the United States. Then we have to source it domestically and ship it back to China. That little connector accumulates a lot of unnecessary cost (and miles) by going through so many layers of distribution. Plus, all that shipping becomes a point of vulnerability to delivery issues. Most of the time, there's a

Chinese equivalent that's as good or better, saving cost and significant component lead time.

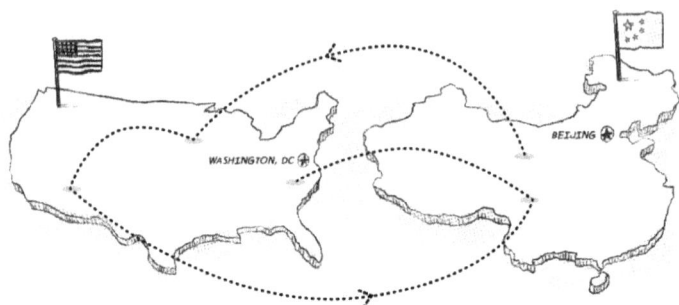

We believe in supporting our customers long term, so we never obsolete anything we build as long as we can get the components for it. We try to steer our customers toward subcomponents with the greatest availability and longevity so we don't wind up at the mercy of the market later on. A good supplier should always consider their own supply chain when they collaborate with you on a new design.

EFFECTIVE COLLABORATION

It's easy to lose perspective during the design process. When you have so many details to keep track of, you have to constantly refer back to the concrete reality of how your product will look, feel, and function in the real world. That's why I advise display customers to use mock-ups from the beginning and samples or demos as soon as possible.

One of our past clients was creating a piece of financial equipment that would display content in Chinese and Japanese characters. They wanted an incredibly high-resolution display because they had a limited amount of space to show a fairly large amount of text, and these characters are pretty intricate with significant detail, requiring this higher resolution.

We went to great lengths to give them the highest pixel density possible, really designing to the extreme limits of LCD technology. When we were finally getting close to the point where the customer was satisfied with the results, I took a step back.

I stopped and printed the sample content on paper at the same resolution and scale of the final display. The display was accomplishing the objective of rendering fine detail with such high pixel density, but it was way too small to read. This product was also intended to be viewed from a distance, and the text was so tiny that you couldn't distinguish anything from more than a few inches away. We'd gone through so much of the design process but lost touch with the basics.

Plan your content on paper first. It's so easy to first create images of everything you want to include on a display—whether that's text, alerts, a go/no-go button, or any graphical user interface that you envision for this product. Simply print it out on paper using the same colors and resolution that you're working with in spec. Then literally tape it to your product, stand back, and look. You'll learn a lot without going through the effort and expense of tooling or producing prototypes.

After you've (hopefully) eliminated all the low-hanging fruit and are ready to see your components in action, talk to your supplier about whether they can provide you with basic samples or full demos. When you receive a sample, you still have to wire it up and figure out how to communicate with it.

With a demo, your supplier can probably load the demo with samples of your own content so all you need to do is supply power. Then you can walk around, look at it from different angles, and get a much better sense of how it will function inside your product.

Effective design comes from collaboration. You and your supplier need to cooperate and share ideas in order to uncover problems or misunderstandings and watch each other's blind spots. The right supplier will give you many different tools to visualize and experience the way their component can enhance your end product.

FROM DESIGN TO PRODUCTION

By the end of your design process, you'll know whether you're working with a supplier who is good at design. But the world's greatest design is useless if the vendor can't actually ship the products as they are designed. Your interactions with the supplier throughout the stages of design, prototypes, or perhaps even qualification will give you a good sense for the type of supplier that you are dealing with. There are so many steps and opportunities to either delight or disappoint clients throughout this process. Relationships are all about the little things. Long-term relationships are based on successful short-term steps. Back in Chapter 3, we talked about assessing a vendor's ability to deliver by looking at how timely and responsive they are during the quote process. The same holds true here.

A supplier who is diligent, helpful, and thorough at identifying your needs will bring those same qualities to the production process. A supplier who is proactive and collaborative during the design phase is demonstrating how they will communicate with you throughout your relationship. As you proceed through the tooling, revisions, and qualification phases, you'll see their organization in action. When a supplier delivers timely, high-quality work in their samples, it's an indication (but not a guarantee) that they can do the same with your finished parts. The converse is true as well. If your supplier struggles to deliver in the design or sample phase, there should be some concern about their capabilities in mass production. This entire process is a long drawn-out test that relates to how well this supplier will support you in the next phases of the relationship.

Find out if your supplier supports pilot volumes. A pilot phase is usually anywhere between fifteen to one hundred units. You don't want to build out a thousand units at this point. There's a good chance you'll find opportunities during the small lot builds and testing that reveal ways the component could be improved. If you're forced to build in higher volume MOQs and you need to make a component change as a result of your pilot build, there would be a lot of waste. It is important to know up front if the supplier won't run less than a thousand units for your product ramp-up phase.

Approaching a supplier about your new product is a bit like a blind date. You know yourself and your needs, but you don't know anything about the other person yet. The process of design and preparation is your opportunity to get to know your partner. There will be many steps along the way that build your confidence in their abilities and their commitment. By the time you're ready to go into production, you will know them very well, and you'll both be ready for a long productive partnership.

TAKE IT TO THE NEXT LEVEL

A longtime customer of ours wanted to create an entirely new
design with a new set of their industry standard requirements.
They were building a server that would live in a room packed
full of their servers. One of their new requirements was the
ability to withstand a much higher ESD (electrostatic discharge)
specification. There are a lot of opportunities for ESD in a server
room, so the new extreme ESD tolerance was essential.

We started off with typical methods, like adding a lot of ground
planes to distribute the electrical charge. But all this did was

give the ESD charge a more optimal path directly into the controller IC chip, which would then stall out the product. That resulted in a complete product failure, and the device would then need to be manually reset each time. Our design improvements had completely backfired.

We took a visit to the customer's site so we could see exactly what they were doing and work directly with their design and integration team. Our strategy was to direct the static electricity around the display instead of trying to distribute the energy through the ground planes of the display. While working with our client's design team, we were able to identify some additional clearance in front of the display. We used this space to add an additional layer of conductive glass on the very front of the LCD display. We then grounded this front conductive glass directly to the chassis of their product through the attachment methods they were already using. The result was a modification to our LCD product that didn't require any modification to the customer's end product at all. And the net result allowed the static charge to flow around the display and dissipate in the body of the server instead of going through our LCD IC and causing a display fault.

By integrating the ground path into the glass and the existing mounts of the display itself, we were able to simplify the overall design and exceed their new, stricter ESD specifications by more than 50 percent in a cost-efficient way. The best part was that this new product opened up additional markets for the customer, and we got the privilege and the bonus of additional volumes for helping them accomplish it.

Your goal should be to obtain the most efficient system-level solution, and therefore, your supplier's goal should be the same. But they can't achieve that goal without diving into the whole system to help you get there. That means balancing system-level costs (including quality) with performance, longevity, and manufacturability. It also means reducing your risks of all five supply chain problems. The right supplier will not only invest in your future profitability, but they will benefit from it as well. The next-level supplier understands that your success is their success, too.

CHAPTER 8

BUILDING A NEXT-LEVEL PARTNERSHIP

I learned the hard way that the customer is always right.

Early on in building this business, we had a customer who makes electronic card readers for video games. They were using a unique glass platform, and after several years, that format was becoming less and less common. In order to keep our customer's configuration stable for as long as possible, we created safety stock of that glass.

Because it wasn't a popular size, we were looking at larger minimum order requirements. We had to buy 5,000 pieces at a time. I made the customer pay for the safety stock we were holding, and we had to pass on the higher MOQs, too.

The customer was frustrated, but I believed I was doing the right thing to keep them from going line-down. So despite their reservations, I held them to those requirements. After several conversations about the situation, they got so frustrated that they eventually found another supplier who had better terms for this display. They were able to lower their MOQ and avoid tying up their capital for all the extra safety stock.

You know what? They were right. I assumed I had the best solution and they would just have to deal with my terms, when I should have put in more effort to solve their problem. I could have had our supply chain team find an alternate glass source or negotiated better with our current source. We should have solved the cost and delivery problems and not let somebody else do it for us.

I learned that the customer is always right, and they proved it. When you decide the customer is wrong, they'll simply stop being your customer. As a supplier, it's my job to build and maintain a positive, mutually beneficial relationship with my customers.

BUILDING TRUST

Choosing a new supplier is a huge commitment, and it requires a lot of trust. This always feels like the standard textbook relationship buzzword when I say it. We are always hearing you need trust and communication in any relationship. I've heard it so much that I don't actually listen to it anymore. But when I think of the actual implications of this trust, I am constantly humbled by how much trust our clients are in fact giving us.

It's not just us—any single supplier that is being used in your assembly has so much impact on your success. For my particular commodity of LCD displays, if I stop supplying as expected (for any one of the myriad reasons), the semi-custom nature of our products will have our customer in a line-down situation for over six months. So for six-plus months, our customer will no longer be able to ship and meet their commitments. That is such a significant impact to any business that I am still humbled each time our clients kick off a new project with us. When you know what to look for, you can find the right supplier who will deserve your trust and keep it for the long term.

Our oldest customer has been with us for sixteen years, and for reference, our average project typically lasts ten years. We focus on long-term relationships with our customers because we aim for system-level success—not just Phoenix Display's success. We're looking to make the customer successful at every step of the process. Full disclosure: This sounds selfless, but it is actually much better for us in the long term as well.

Building trust starts with being heard. I see this with my kids sometimes—they'll come to me frustrated about a problem, and I'll jump straight to telling them where they went wrong and how they should fix it. Of course, they just get more frustrated. Why? Because I skipped a step.

I made a bunch of assumptions in order to give them my feedback, and it doesn't even matter whether any of those assumptions are correct or not. I didn't actually listen, so as a result, they didn't feel heard. They didn't feel like I understood their true problems and situation, nor did they feel like I cared enough to slow down and just listen. Instead, they are going to feel like I'm selling them my best advice or solution but not what might be best for them. The outcome might be exactly the same (especially with my kids because I am always right), but without feeling heard, they don't trust my advice, and they probably won't follow it.

The same is true in supplier relationships. Unless you are confident that your supplier really hears you, you won't believe they fully understand your position or that their recommendations are reliable. Without that confidence and trust, you're much less likely to find the ideal system-level solution.

When you talk to a new supplier, do they listen? Or do they swoop in with a bunch of prepackaged assumptions and solutions?

Some suppliers hand you more problems. Have you ever taken

your car in for an oil change and had the mechanic hit you with "By the way…"? By the way, you need a new air filter. By the way, your timing belt will probably need changing this year. By the way, the tread on those tires is looking low."

Are they even changing the oil? Is any of this true or relevant? You just needed a simple fix, and now you apparently have a broken-down car and a massive headache. When a vendor piles on problems without listening, it undermines your confidence and makes you feel like you're just there to be upsold no matter what.

Another great example is buying a car. A lesser salesman will jump right in telling you how great the vehicle is that you happen to be standing in front of and how amazing all its features are. The great salesman starts instead by asking questions. He listens to you so he can learn which automotive features will actually improve your life.

A good partner builds trust by hearing you out and then responds timely and with your best interest on every task you give them. The right supplier will offer you a path to a better situation than you were in before.

Throughout this book, we've looked at the importance of good alignment with your supplier in terms of volume, industry, and your relative significance to their business. There are three more aspects of alignment that can make or break your partnership: their expertise, their past projects, and their communication.

EXPERTISE

Your supplier's experience with your product type and market are critical. They make the difference between luck and intention: are you going to luck into a great design, or will you intentionally create one?

I have a perfect real-world example going on right now in my own life. I'm right in the middle of a massive yearlong remodeling project at my house. It's awful, of course, but hiring the right person to do the work gave me some new insight into the importance of aligning with a vendor's expertise.

I'm not a house builder or a contractor. I know next to nothing about the process or options that go into renovating a house. I'm not an interior designer either, so I don't have an exact vision of what I want everything to look like. I just know I want the end result to be amazing.

I got a list of contractors to quote my project, and they're all qualified. They're fully capable of getting the job done. So then I dug a little deeper to find out more about their typical projects and their specialties.

The first guy does a lot of high-end multifamily apartment buildings. He's working on big structures and definitely has experience in managing large, complex projects. However, because he's building in volume, he needs to build very economically. That usually translates into an expertise with lower-end commercial materials.

The next guy builds tract homes. So that's a little closer to my needs because he's building single-family homes and he's great with framing and installing materials. But he's building from scratch instead of remodeling, and he's also working with large-volume, lower-budget materials because that's how tract developments work. Also, his finish selection is going to be on the more economical side.

The third guy is a kitchen and bath remodeler. He really understands the important parts of a house, how to design them, and how to upgrade the finishes and appliances. He's got the right sources and works in the right quantities. So we're getting warmer. But the downside with this guy is that my project also involves a lot of framing. He doesn't have the right amount of experience with a significant portion of my project.

Finally, I have a remodel and reconstruction designer. He creates the design, hires out specialty contractors for the different aspects of the work, and oversees the project. He understands high-end finishes and has the network and sources to really support the end result that I'm looking for.

All the vendors were competent and quoted me reasonable prices and time frames. But only one could give expert guidance to an amateur like me, had the specialty that aligned perfectly with my needs, and had the track record to back it up.

Finding alignment with a vendor is much the same for your business. I'm not psychic, so I don't know your company's mission statement, but I'm willing to bet it isn't "Get the job done adequately." It's probably more about creating the best product or experience for your client. In order to do that, you need to find the vendor who is best aligned with you.

PAST PROJECTS

Testimonials from other customers can give you helpful information when it comes to gauging alignment, but I wouldn't advise you to take them at face value. After all, you aren't shopping on Amazon, where you see all the positive, neutral, and negative reviews from the market. A vendor is only going to share testimonials from happy customers. The point here is not to determine if their work was good or not. Instead, use the testimonials to try and figure out what your supplier specializes in. You have to read between the lines to find out what you need to know about the vendor's experience in particular niches of the market that might be a good match to yours. Let's look at some examples, and again, take them with a grain of salt.

One of our customers, GE Healthcare, said:

> In the medical industry, we could not afford to re-qualify our product around an alternate display. Phoenix Display came in with a carefully designed exact match to the display that had been obsoleted by our previous supplier. We found that once in produc-

tion, the quality was even higher with the PDI display as well. We transition a second display to PDI with the same results.

So the useful information there is prior experience in the medical industry, successful cross-matching an obsolete product, and that this is a return customer.

Another example would be Hypercom:

> Phoenix Display has been a critical contributor to our ability to deliver high volume point of sale terminal systems to our market. Their capability to control quality and costs as well as support our rapid changes in demand convinced us to continue with Phoenix Display on twelve different LCD platforms.

The potential points of alignment here are industrial products, high volume, and flexibility to accommodate changes in volume. There's also some information about the type of relationship since the customer continued for twelve different platforms.

Iridium Satellite Phone had this to say:

> As a result of long lead-times and missed schedule commitments from our original LCD supplier, we reached out to Phoenix Display. Phoenix Display customized a 100% identical display to our original display, which was critical as we could not make any changes to our product at this mature stage. PDI was able to meet our schedule demands so we could once again begin to consistently meet our end customer commitments, while reducing our display cost as well.

This one demonstrates the Cross-Match Process again and

has additional information about matching a mature product and reducing costs as well as meeting a tight schedule. You should always look at supplier testimonials with a critical eye, but they can give you some helpful data points to assess how well the vendor is aligned with your product and your current situation.

COMMUNICATION

You also need great communication with your supply partner. In order to collaborate effectively, you need education about their process and about any new factors that could affect them or you. You're planning for a ten- or fifteen-year relationship, so you set expectations at the beginning and then commit to them. Naturally, unexpected things are going to happen. Designs change. Schedules change. When we encounter a deviation, we have to be transparent and forthright about what's happening and how it might impact our customers so they can adjust.

We need the same transparency back from our customers. They might push out a deadline or pull it in closer. They might make design changes after we've built the product. So transparency is important at every stage of the process. You can tell a lot about your partner's communication over the next ten years by looking at how it was up front.

If your communication isn't going well during the supplier selection phase, it's a great indicator that it's probably not going to go well in the design phase either. And if communication leaves a lot to be desired through all these initial phases, again, it's not going to suddenly improve when you reach mass production—when you have the most at stake.

A supplier who is interested in a long-term relationship will tell you when they can't help you. If you show up ready to change suppliers and you're already paying the right price for the right quality and performance, your parts are available and delivered on time, then there's nothing I can do for you. All I can do is validate that you're doing a great job. I can't solve any problems for you because you don't actually have any of the five problems.

The supplier should also give you feedback about whether you're a good fit for them. As I mentioned at the beginning of this book, we refer about 90 percent of potential customers to someone else. Our whole business model is based on the ability to work with customers who are the best fit for us so we can give all of them top-quality service.

When you and your supplier are well aligned and they're fully prepared to meet your needs, your conversations should be easy (or at least, they shouldn't be hard). From the initial call, they should help you navigate their process so that you leave every interaction knowing more than you did before and with greater confidence of success on your project. They should always give you a clear understanding of the next step you need to take.

TRUST THE PROCESS

When you walk up to the counter at Starbucks, every barista is trained to ask one question: "Hi, what can I get started for you?"

You've entered a business process. It's clear, it's simple, and it makes your life as a customer so much easier. They could ask, "How was your day?" or "Can I help you?" But that would just create noise. You know they don't really care about your day. You wouldn't be there if they couldn't help you. It would slow you down and put the onus on you to get the transaction underway.

Instead, they show that they're already on it—you want coffee, and they're ready to make it. It's very kind and courteous, but there's no messing around. Your experience is on rails, and you don't have to think about anything except what you want. Working with a supplier should be the same way. A great supplier has a clear process that guides your experience in working with them.

Working with a vendor who doesn't have a robust process is like playing charades. You're constantly guessing at what things mean, or you're trying very hard to communicate and the other person just can't seem to understand. It's frustrating, and often you can't get to your goal.

When a supplier doesn't have a well-designed process or they aren't transparent about it, it's confusing for you as the customer. You may be left wondering what the next step should be. Are they going to call with the information, or should you follow up? What are the timelines? How, exactly, are you supposed to work together? Most importantly, how can you ensure you're getting the best results?

What if you don't even know exactly what you want? You're an expert in your product, but you aren't an expert in every single component or subcomponent. You shouldn't have to be! It's the supplier's job to guide you through your options and help you find the best solution for your product.

Think of buying your first home stereo system. You know what it does and you have some idea how it works in a general way, but you aren't an expert on all the different equipment options, the acoustics, the best way to set everything up—and you don't want to be. You just want some music in your house. You have no clue what that means in terms of specifications—Do you need more speakers? Bigger speakers? Better speakers? More power? Different input options? Remote control capabilities? What frequency range capability do you need? Who knows?

The seller knows. But before you even get to those details, you have to decide where to go. Should you be shopping at a big-box store like Target, at an electronics store like Best Buy, or at a high-end custom retailer that caters to audiophiles? You might pick one, but the seller should immediately invite you into the process to define what you're really looking for. The first thing they need to confirm is whether you're in the right store. If you need a system bigger than anything they can provide or your budget is smaller than they can work with, a good supplier will send you somewhere else. That's the best outcome for both of you.

When you find the right match, your seller can begin to guide you further. Their process should systematically discover your needs and expectations and then translate them into specifications for the precise product that will deliver what you want.

Our businesses all work the same way. You start by knowing what kind of customer you are and have an idea of what kind of supplier you're looking for. The supplier will know this even better and should have a very clear process to confirm that it's a good match. If so, they should guide you through each step to define your needs and how they can help.

Our process starts with simple questions: "What made you call us? Was it one of the five problems or a new opportunity?" Then we learn about what's going on today and why things are different than yesterday. We listen to your problems and then walk you down the path of solving them.

When you vet a supplier's process, look at their willingness to solve problems and their ability to execute those solutions. On the one hand, a supplier who's really aligned with you should be willing to work around your needs and find the most effective way to integrate their components into your product. The question becomes, do they have the capability to make that happen?

Can they create custom solutions? Are they using leading-edge technology? Do they have in-house design teams who can make changes? Do they have their own prototype labs to give you samples along the way? If you're looking for a vendor who will give top-level service, make sure they can actually perform at that level.

We realized early on that the majority of our business consisted of solving one or more of the five supply chain problems. About 65 percent of our clients come to us due to problems with their current supplier. All this practice led us to formulate a very specific process around creating replacements for their existing product. Whether the underlying problem is logistics, technology, or availability, once we've demonstrated to the customer that we can overcome that issue, the process remains the same. Your next supplier's process may vary in some ways, but it should be robust and thorough, and they should lay it out clearly for you from the beginning.

THE CROSS-MATCH PROCESS

CROSSMATCH PROGRAM TIMELINE

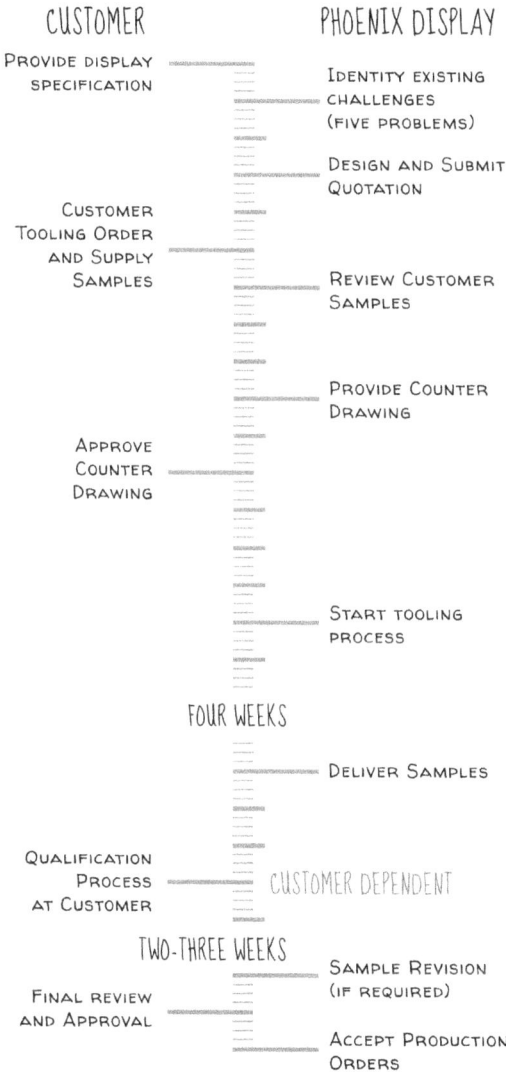

CUSTOMER	PHOENIX DISPLAY

PROVIDE DISPLAY
SPECIFICATION

IDENTITY EXISTING
CHALLENGES
(FIVE PROBLEMS)

DESIGN AND SUBMIT
QUOTATION

CUSTOMER
TOOLING ORDER
AND SUPPLY
SAMPLES

REVIEW CUSTOMER
SAMPLES

PROVIDE COUNTER
DRAWING

APPROVE
COUNTER
DRAWING

START TOOLING
PROCESS

FOUR WEEKS

DELIVER SAMPLES

QUALIFICATION
PROCESS
AT CUSTOMER

CUSTOMER DEPENDENT

TWO-THREE WEEKS

SAMPLE REVISION
(IF REQUIRED)

FINAL REVIEW
AND APPROVAL

ACCEPT PRODUCTION
ORDERS

TYPICAL LEAD TIME IS FIVE–EIGHT WEEKS TOTAL
FOR INITIAL QUALIFICATION UNITS

The goal of our Cross-Match Process is to create a replacement part that is completely compatible with the customer's existing product configuration so they don't have to make any changes on their end. This is an internal process specific to our company, but I'm sharing it with you in order to illustrate the type of system any supplier would need to have in place in order to provide a tailored solution specific to a new client's needs.

If the customer is forced to alter their end product in order to accommodate a replacement component, it involves engineering and tooling their end product for this new configuration. Then they have to deal with managing the old and new configurations, which creates problems with marketing and product returns. All in all, it's much more expensive to accommodate any component changes, so we try to add as much value to our customers as possible by eliminating those changes.

Occasionally, when a subcomponent is truly gone forever, we may wind up with a replacement part that requires some software updates or patches in order to function seamlessly. In an even more rare instance, the nearest possible solution might require hardware changes like a different pin-out. That might mean a different electrical circuit or a new printed circuit board. We try to avoid that type of situation whenever possible, but even those minor changes are better than a customer canceling their end product because they can no longer manufacture it.

Our commitment throughout the Cross-Match Process is to take as much off the customer's plate as possible and really make it easy for them. Let me walk you through the steps from initial quote to mass production.

THE QUOTE

To start a quote, we need display specifications from the customer. In a few cases (like the military contractor I mentioned in Chapter 1), we don't have written specifications and need to draw them up ourselves from a physical specimen. That's certainly more challenging, but if that's all we have available, we can do it.

With or without the written specifications, we prefer to get a sample part to examine. That way, we can fully analyze all the physical and performance attributes and retain it for comparison testing later. We also take into account all the information we gathered from the customer during our initial discussions about volume, timelines, cost, and which of the five problems we're trying to solve for them. We do our initial design work and submit a quote.

THE DESIGN PHASE

Once the customer accepts the quote and commits to the tooling order, we can go more in depth on the design work. If we didn't receive samples during the quote phase, it is helpful to get them now.

We review those samples and look for anything that might not be listed in the specifications. We use them to do precise matching for attributes that can be hard to capture in specifications, like the particular color of glass and the visual effect of the way it combines with the backlight. Or contrast—specifications will state the ratio between dark and light, but how dark is the dark? The same contrast ratio can look very different with a different color baseline. We need to see the samples and compare them to really be able to fully color match and duplicate a component.

Our goal is to create a replacement that's indistinguishable from the original part. If a customer walks into their warehouse with racks full of units, we don't want them to be able to see that one unit was produced by Supplier A and the other by Supplier B.

We use this analysis to create a formal counter-drawing that documents the detailed design of the new part. The customer may approve the counter-drawing, or there might be some iterations here. They may notice something that needs refinement, or they may have an idea that would help the product be even more efficient than the original design. We work through those iterations and proceed to tool up for production.

It's still possible to make design changes once we start the tooling process, but there may be cost implications. From tooling, we can typically deliver samples to the client within four to eight weeks.

Here again, there's an opportunity for iteration if changes to the sample are necessary. We might see interferences that didn't show up in the original design analysis, or we might identify ways to improve the product's efficiency or manufacturability (we looked at some of those possibilities in Chapter 6). Most of the time, no changes are needed at this stage, but in about 15 to 20 percent of cases, we'll see something that could be improved. It's not typical, but I would never proceed into the production phase without waiting for potential revisions.

QUALIFICATION AND PRODUCTION

If everything looks good, the next step is the customer's testing and qualification process. Of course, the timeline for that depends on the customer, but we usually anticipate about two to three weeks. There's one more opportunity for sample revision if the testing turns up any need for changes or room for improvement.

Customer qualification processes can vary a lot. I've been shocked by how quickly some consumer products move through this phase. I'll send samples, they'll put it in a device, and away they go. With others, especially automotive customers, they might put them in a burn-in rack and test them for several weeks (sometimes months).

There's dimensional analysis—we do that on our end, but some customers repeat it to check every dimension against the specifications. Customer testing can also include end product drop testing from one or two meters onto all six sides, and exposure to extreme environmental factors like heat, humidity, and temperature cycling for prolonged periods.

Just as with new product design, some customers like to run a pilot program of fifty to one hundred units in order to get feedback from the assembly workers, update their operating instructions, and look for any additional interfaces from variation in tolerance stack-ups. Sometimes we'll see a replacement part that appears to be a seamless match in every way, but in assembly, we'll discover interference between the new part and a manufacturing assembly fixture. Then we need to determine whether it makes more sense to change the component or for the customer to change their fixture. We always want to find the most efficient solution.

From there, we move to final review and approval by the customer. Once the configuration is approved, we can accept a purchase order for production quantities. The typical time from initial quote to delivery of qualification units is five to eight weeks, but it can vary quite a bit depending on the design time and the customer's internal processes.

Often when our customers come to us, they believe they're ready to go, the design will be quick, and they'll say they need the component in four weeks. We'll do our best to expedite the process, but I always try to give them realistic expectations. In my experience, we'll uncover one issue after another as we go through the design for all the subcomponents. Integrating design changes from every single subcomponent is a complex process, and trying to rush through never pays off in the end.

Going through our process systematically allows us to be successful with our clients' projects 100 percent of the time. I know that sounds boastful or too good to be true. The key is knowing how to say no to the wrong clients so that we can give 100 percent of our yeses to the right clients. We place such a high value on customer alignment because we are fully committed to our customers' success—which is the driver of our success.

COMMITTED TO YOUR SUCCESS

The right supplier won't just hand off your component. They will take ownership of the end result.

I think anyone in business has, at some point, encountered coworkers, employees, or vendors who don't think beyond the task at hand. If I ask an employee to check pricing on a new connector and their response at the results meeting is, "I sent an email and never heard back," we have a problem. This is a small-scale example, but I didn't ask for an email. I asked for pricing.

The same holds true for client deliverables. The client wanted a new component that seamlessly integrates with their already designed and in-production end product. Not an incompatibility accompanied by a statement that "this is the specification we agreed to." If we don't achieve the desired result, we haven't succeeded because we didn't make the customer successful.

We give our customers a guarantee that we won't invoice them if they're not happy. Let me reiterate that. *If you put your product through our cross-match program and you aren't happy with the result, we won't invoice you.* This is an easy guarantee for us to make because we've never had that happen. Occasionally, we run up against limitations—like the laws of physics or when a subcomponent is obsolete and we had to accommodate a variance. But so far, our customers have been satisfied that we've matched their parts as far as humanly possible.

The goal is to create the best possible end product and the most profitable situation for the customer. Success isn't about meeting specifications—it's building a partnership that brings the customer's business to the next level. That's the best way to build relationships that last.

You consider changing suppliers because you're in a painful situation. Change is painful, too, so you're only going to make the move when the pain of change is less than the pain of your current problem. The risk you always face is that you might walk out of one painful situation and into a new one that's even worse. If you're stuck with obsolescence, you have no choice but to change—but did you walk into a delivery or quality problem? Will you wind up trapped in a sneaky cost problem because the supplier lowballed you but makes a lot of price increases?

The right supplier will address all five problems with you up front. They can show you the mitigation plans and contingencies they have in place to protect you. A supplier with potential for a next-level relationship will take the initiative to make change easier and less painful for you. The right supplier isn't just out to sell you some components. A next-level partner will invest in your long-term success.

CONCLUSION

Why change?

I wrote this book so that you could answer that question for yourself. After reading it, hopefully you should be clear about the reasons why you need a new component supplier or why not. Of course, all my personal examples relate to LCD displays because that's my business and what I'm familiar with. No matter what type of electronic components you're sourcing, the same principles still apply. You should have a number of practical strategies for working with your existing supplier to shore up weaknesses in your supply chain before they become insurmountable. And you should now have a strong framework for vetting new suppliers who can become trusted partners.

For most buyers and engineers, it's not your job to go out and find new suppliers on a regular basis. Your ordinary responsibilities are all about working with the suppliers you already have. Making those connections and exploring those new options take up a lot of bandwidth. The devil you know is easier to deal with than the devil you don't.

The sunk-cost fallacy is a huge deterrent to engineers and purchasing managers investigating their options in the supply chain. When you've invested time, energy, and money into a supplier relationship, it's hard to be completely rational and logical about assessing it. In investing terms, when the value of your investment goes down, it's human nature to hope that we can recoup that value by holding on. But the past value doesn't always predict the future value of that investment. You have to look at the situation dispassionately and determine whether your investment is likely to make gains or go down further. Sometimes you need to cut your losses and reinvest in a different place.

When you thoroughly understand your own needs as a customer, you can accurately assess the risks in your supply chain and find the right partner to help you move forward and grasp new opportunities. That applies to all five of the supply chain problems as well as the risks inherent in new product development.

There are so many creative solutions available to overcome an obsolescence situation that you don't need to throw your hands up and declare an impasse. Instead of being constantly frustrated by slow or missing deliveries, you can raise the water in your supply chain and sail over those obstacles. With the right supplier, you can set high expectations for quality and performance without wasting resources. You can validate your costs—or reduce them—by asking suppliers to address your system-level burdens instead of focusing on price per unit. And when it's time to develop a new product, make sure you're also addressing the five problems so you can choose a partner who brings more to the table than you thought to ask for.

The answer to every one of these problems is alignment. Vendors give the most attention and service to their most important customers—that's only natural. The question is, how do you become one of those important customers?

When you find the right match on industry, volume, and distribution, you can build a strong relationship with that supplier. That alignment turns a vendor into a partner who really listens to your needs and concerns, looks for ways to add value to your product, and invests in your success.

If you're wrestling with a complex problem in your supply chain and need more insight, we have videos and articles available on our website with even more in-depth information on the five problems and different ways to approach them. You can find those resources on our blog at phoenixdisplay.com.

On the site, you'll also find a request form so you can get in touch. You can email us with any questions you may have, or just pick up the phone and give us a call. As I've mentioned, we refer out the majority of our inquiries because we want to make sure that both of us are finding the right fit, and we're always happy to help with that.

Change is painful and expensive. Ultimately, the only reason to change is when the pain point in your supply chain is worse than the pain of change. I'm humbled by the amount of trust my customers put into our organization. I know how difficult it is to change and how much there is at stake. It takes a lot of time and resources to change course, so you have to make a long-term commitment just to get started. Then if things don't work out down the road, it's a long and painful process to start over again with someone new.

Picking the wrong supplier can cause a lot of damage to your business, so there's a lot of value to finding the best match. The right supply partner makes change easier. Finding that partner can take your product and your business to a whole new level. I hope this book helps you reach that next level in your partnerships and your own success.

ABOUT THE AUTHOR

KEITH MITNIK is the co-founder of Phoenix Display, an LCD display company. With a background in mechanical engineering and a master's degree in business, Keith has applied his expertise to identify the patterns and solve problems in supply chain management for the past two decades.

A quest to find clients who were a perfect fit for the company developed into a comprehensive business philosophy that proper alignment between client and vendor delivers the most value to both parties. Over twenty years of practice, that philosophy produced a practical model clients can follow to find the vendor who is a perfect fit for them.

This book documents Keith's clear framework for customers to resolve issues with current suppliers, determine when and how to change to new suppliers, manage the transitional process, and ensure sustainable success.

www.ingramcontent.com/pod-product-compliance
Lightning Source LLC
Chambersburg PA
CBHW031851200326
41597CB00012B/371